W9-DFB-726

WITH GLADNESS
Answering God's Call
in Our Everyday Lives

WITH GLADNESS
Answering God's Call
in Our Everyday Lives

Christopher H. Martin

FORWARD MOVEMENT
Cincinnati, Ohio

About the cover: The mosaic ceiling of the Florence Baptistery.

Scripture quotations are from the New Revised Standard Version of the Bible, copyright © 1989 National Council of the Churches of Christ in the United States of America. Used by permission. All rights reserved.

Psalm passages are from the Psalter in *The Book of Common Prayer.*

© 2020 Forward Movement
All rights reserved.
ISBN: 978-0-88028-496-7
Printed in USA

Forward
Movement
inspire disciples. empower evangelists.

For the people of
St. Paul's Episcopal Church
in San Rafael, California

Table of Contents

Introduction

You are body and soul.

I make that claim about you because I am a Christian. An atheist would say that you are just a body, and the word "soul" is a kind of metaphor for a bunch of chemicals combining to produce thoughts and feelings. No God, no soul. But a Christian believes that she is body and soul, and while one ceases to function at our earthly death, the other, in a way that is still mysterious to us, can, by grace, continue eternally with God. While the glory of life eternal is a gift incomprehensible, I wonder if we can we live now in such a way that we get a foretaste of this eternal life with God. Can we love and serve God now with gladness and singleness of heart?

This book emerges from a failure to answer that question well. For nearly a decade, I have been building and developing a renewal movement called The Restoration Project. This movement is centered on the practices of prayer, worship, and service, with small-group gatherings nurturing people as disciples of Jesus. While the movement inspired people across the country to grow in spiritual depth, I hit a roadblock in February of 2018. The Restoration Project team hosted a gathering of forty people from around the country who were either already in Discipleship Groups or wanting to learn more about them. Discipleship Groups are at the heart of The Restoration Project movement. These small groups are structured for Christian maturity and mission by encouraging seven core Christian practices. Each meeting of a Discipleship Group starts with a liturgy that includes the recitation of seven vows, one for each practice. Over the course of the gathering, we often broke into small groups to discuss, in sequence, each of the seven practices. Six of the seven conversations were inspiring and educational. The one that failed was about "call."

People loved the language of the vow: "By God's grace, I will listen for God's call on my life, confident that I have been 'given a manifestation of the Spirit for the common good'" (1 Corinthians 12:7), entrusting my Discipleship Group to test and support that call." But we kept running into two problems with the vow. The first was that, despite years of effort, those of us leading The Restoration Project in our parishes and dioceses had proven unable to shake the idea that "call" applies only to clergy, monks, nuns, and missionaries. For ordinary lay people, call doesn't really apply, and further, even for clergy, it only applied that one time when we were trying to figure out, with the help of our church, if we should be ordained. After that, the word seemed to be too often discarded. Perhaps we knew in our heads that this wasn't quite true, but when we gathered and faced the opportunity to apply the vow to our own lives, we discovered not only a profound disconnect but also a failure to get any momentum in conversation.

The other problem with the vow was the lack of specificity. Each of the other vows has a specific goal. We are to work toward twenty minutes a day of prayer, an hour a week in service of the poor, giving ten percent to the church and those in need, and some knowledge of the whole of scripture. Each of these is a concrete goal toward which we can work. Although the language in the vow on call was lovely and evocative, it didn't hold us accountable for anything concrete. The vow proved to be a dead end.

This was particularly sad for me because I felt that call was the culminating practice of The Restoration Project. The man who inspired The Restoration Project, Gordon Cosby, taught me that we each have a call and do not come fully alive until we follow it. Further, while there are likely to be similar patterns in our call throughout our lives, call manifests itself in different ways in different seasons of our lives. When we created the liturgy of the Discipleship Groups, the idea was that the other six vows fulfilled their purpose when they pointed to and supported us to go out into the world to do the work God sends us to do. With an ineffective vow on call, we had a machine that was missing its most important part.

After the retreat, the leaders of The Restoration Project, both at my church, St. Paul's in San Rafael, California, and from churches in Nebraska, Indiana, and Florida, began revising the vow and testing it out with a variety of groups. In the spring of 2019, I was invited to St. John's Cathedral in Jacksonville, Florida, to preach and teach on the new vow. We received the affirmation for which we had been hoping. After a church service, I shared some of the material that you will find in this book. I explained the power in the practice of simply naming the work that is before us and trusting that it is work that God has sent us to do. My friend Kate Moorehead, the dean of the cathedral, jumped in and said that her son would be coming back from college in the coming week. Her work—call, if you will—was to establish healthy boundaries for his summer at home and to prepare the room above the garage so that he wasn't forced to sleep in his brother's bedroom.

After the talk was over, a woman came up to both of us with tears in her eyes. This was particularly striking because she had been one of the acolytes in the service, and I noticed and admired her sense of presence, calm, and intentionality, even wearing a knowing and winsome smile as she served. She thanked Kate and me for the teaching and said that when she heard the words call, vocation, or gift, she had an automatic response on the inside that said, "That's not about me, that's not about me." She coupled those words with a firm and clear gesture of pushing something away with her hands. But after our discussion, she understood call in a new way—as the practice of naming ordinary, everyday work and coming to embrace that each work could be done for the glory of God.

This book offers a path for you to identify and answer God's call in your everyday life. In these pages, I share with you a daily prayer and seven gentle practices to help you embrace a new and ancient way of being a Christian in the world, body and soul.

The book can be read either alone or in conjunction with a prayer partner, spiritual director, or small group. I'm seeking a style of writing where, in one sitting, you can read through the chapter and get going on the practice for that week. At the same time, each chapter, with the help of scripture and some profound Christian voices, has enough density that, throughout the week, as you implement the prayer and gentle practice, you can return to the chapter and chew a bit more on what's there.

This process is ideal for use during Lent. If you read the first chapter on Ash Wednesday, you will end up reading the last chapter on the Wednesday of Holy Week, just before entering into the great days of Maundy Thursday, Good Friday, Holy Saturday, and Easter. But it doesn't have to be used in Lent. Anytime you feel ready to focus on the life of your soul such that you would like to move through your ordinary days with gladness and singleness of heart, I encourage you to give this book a try.

Christopher H. Martin

Guiding Principles:
How to Use This Book

As you work through the book, please bear in mind three methods in our way of proceeding. These three methods are words, shifts, and repetitions.

The first method in our process is how we pay attention to words. Each chapter draws focused attention to a small handful of words. Some of them will be familiar, used along the lines of what you might expect. Examples are the words sent, work, and singleness. Other words are given some very specific meanings that are particular to the practices. These are words like sabbath, conviction, and Beauty with a capital B. Part of the practice is like learning a new language. When you're learning Spanish, you look at a dog and think to yourself *perro*, until it becomes second nature and you don't have to make an effort anymore: *perro* comes as easily as the word dog.

We will also proceed with a high respect for the power of words. The Christian poet Samuel Taylor Coleridge wrote, "accustom yourself to reflect on the words you use... for if words are not things, they are living powers, by which things of most importance to (humankind) are actuated, combined and humanized."[1] By slowing down and paying attention to just a few words each week, I invite you to actuate, combine, and humanize the events and the thoughts that occur to you as you move through your days in such a way that you love and serve God with gladness and singleness of heart.

Secondly, it is important to view each of the gentle practices as small and subtle shifts in our souls. Just as a chiropractor or physical therapist might have you practice shifts in the way you hold your head, attend to your low back as you sit, or shift your shoulders as you stand, so these gentle practices improve the posture of your soul. Understanding this method is likely to become increasingly important as you embrace the gentle practices.

For many people, the practices might feel overwhelming. That was Brigitte's experience the first time I taught this material. I had already introduced the daily prayer and two of the gentle practices. Brigitte was trying to do them all and was overwhelmed. It was like walking, chewing gum, rubbing her belly, and patting her head at the same time! When you are working on your body's posture, it often helps to focus on one of the shifts, such as putting your shoulders back. That one focus can then help the other shifts come into place for you. So it is with these prayers and practices. Focus on one at a time and don't get overly concerned about the others at the moment. They are called gentle practices precisely because we can easily get frustrated with ourselves and judgmental about a new effort we are pursuing.

I share these gentle practices in the spirit of the great teacher of centering prayer, Thomas Keating. He repeatedly reminds us that when we sit in silence in Christian meditation, we are to use our prayer word, like the word God or Love, to nudge aside ever-so-gently whatever thought begins to preoccupy us. Likewise, as we move through the course of our ordinary days, we are invited to gently practice improving the posture of our soul as we look at faces, name our work, pray and reflect, smile our secret smile, use our wound, or name our spiritual home. We are invited to do one at a time, particularly the first time we read through this book.

At the same time, these gentle practices are well worth revisiting more than once. Writing this book is now the sixth time that I have shared this material. Each time I revisit it, a different element of the work emerges as the one that draws me in and shifts me. These shifts are happening in two ways. The first is the shift in what I pay attention to and how I pay that attention. For example, in one of the gentle practices, I invite you to pay attention to each human face you see in a different way. We are also invited to experience a shift through our bodies. When we shift our attention to, for example, our side or our mouth, we are reminded to shift the posture of our soul and live with just a bit more gladness and singleness of heart.

Our final method is to be attentive to repetition. A violinist constantly repeats scales, whatever her level of virtuosity, and a ballet dancer constantly repeats basic dance moves with a hand on the bar, whether he is a beginner or part of a professional company. The repetition assures competence and beauty. One great violinist said that if he didn't practice for one day, he could tell. If he didn't practice for two days, an expert could tell. If he didn't practice for three days, everyone could tell. It is the attentive repetition of practice that keeps the beauty fresh.

In my freshman year, I perhaps foolishly volunteered with my friend Adam to be the first to present a scene in an acting class. We chose a scene between Brick and Big Daddy from

Cat on a Hot Tin Roof by Tennessee Williams. Despite a lot of practice, we were terrible. The teacher, who we found out later had worked closely with Williams and had been the director of several of his debuts, was kind. He told us that when Degas painted the legs of a ballerina, he sketched line after line on the paper until he got the line that was just right. We were to rehearse scenes in the same spirit. The lesson was clear. Creating a through-line for a scene for an actor means repeating the scene in rehearsal, finding many different ways from the beginning to the end until it becomes clear how I make the life of that particular character believable and compelling. The words of the scene are the same each time. But movement, gesture, and tone can take on infinitely shaded variation. The repetition of the same lines, for a lively actor, provides not monotony but an infinite invitation to creativity.

So it can be in our real lives. Our lives are filled with repetitions. We drive the same routes, exchange pleasantries with the same people, and are given the same daily tasks. The art is to discover and claim what theologian and poet Catherine Pickstock calls the gift of "the happy ability to vary the quotidian, to take delight in the subtle variations of day after day shared with friends, or with a marriage partner."[2] It is in a new alertness to these "day after day" repetitions that we begin to improve the posture of our souls.

Just as you stand strong when your feet are planted and walk well when you attend to a healthy stride, so the posture of our soul begins with a metaphor about our feet. To begin our traverse of this book and its practices, I invite you to put on Camino boots. In 2010, one of my best friends and I agreed to walk the ancient Christian pilgrimage of the Camino. The most popular version of the Camino has pilgrims cross north Spain, westward bound to Santiago de Campostela, where the church remembers that the bones of Saint James the Apostle lie. We diligently researched and found many places online with advice about how to prepare and what to pack. All sources were united in one piece of advice: you must break in your boots before you begin the Camino. My Camino buddy bought the boots in plenty of time but didn't have the opportunity to break them in properly. Sure enough, by day four, his feet were a blistery wreck, and we traveled half our usual distance at half our usual speed while his feet got tough, and his boots got soft. By the end of the Camino, we were capable of long days of strong and joyful walking.

The two boots for your soul are worship and prayer. When these two are well-worn into your life, you can more easily embrace the gentle practices. Worship means praying with people every Sunday. For the purposes of this book, weekly worship is an expected part of your spiritual life; the power of the sabbath prayer and reflection will help you integrate the five gentle practices.

Prayer means twenty minutes of solitary prayer each day. The twenty minutes a day is neither arbitrary nor prescriptive. Research shows that people who pray for twenty minutes or more a day express a much higher level of satisfaction with their prayer life than those who pray less than that. We are specific about the minimum time spent, but what you do with that time is between you and God. After teaching prayer for more than two decades, I have found that almost everyone has a baseline practice of either centering prayer or some other variation of Christian meditation or Morning Prayer as found in *The Book of Common Prayer*. Your creative work is to find a way of prayer that works for you and then, in the words of the great spiritual director, Abbot John Chapman, to "pray as you can, and don't try and pray as you can't."[3]

The work of improving the posture of your soul begins with concluding your prayer time each day with prayer. The first chapter introduces a prayer, explains it, and then invites you to pray it each day, alongside a gentle practice of reminding yourself that the work is very near you. Chapters two and three introduce the gentle practices to look at each face and name each work. In chapter four, the gentle practice is to pray and reflect on the sabbath. The sabbath prayer invites reflection such that the gentle practices start to integrate themselves into our body and soul. In weeks five and six, I introduce two more gentle practices. These gentle practices are both more subtle and more profound than the first two. Find your secret smile and use your wounds to touch on and transfigure our sense of truth and reality.

In the final chapter, you are invited to name your spiritual center and with beautiful posture and graceful strength in your body and soul, to march each day toward that great goal. It invites us to imagine that we have, through the weeks of embracing these practices, changed from being disciples to being pilgrims, people who are on the Way with Jesus toward what we know is our spiritual center.

CHAPTER ONE
The Work Is Very Near You

GENTLE PRACTICE

In times of transition, think to yourself:
"The work is very near you."

WORDS

Work   Send
Gentle

O God, send me this day to do the work
you have given me to do,
to love and serve you with
gladness and singleness of heart. Amen.

The Work Is Very Near You

We begin by introducing prayer into our daily life. Prayer helps introduce the gentle practices into our bodies and so into our lives. The daily prayer is composed of the two post-communion prayers in Rite II of *The Book of Common Prayer*. This daily prayer takes sentences we ordinarily apply to the coming week and applies them to the day before us. The prayer is:

> *O God, send me this day to do the work you have given me to do, to love and serve you with gladness and singleness of heart.* Amen.

There are many powerful words in this prayer, and throughout this chapter, we will unpack these words, a process that will continue in the weeks and chapters to come.

The first word we will unpack is "work," which is at the heart of the occasional prayer. In the Bible, the book of Deuteronomy is presented as a series of sermons Moses gives to the people of Israel. The Israelites have made it through forty years in the wilderness and are on the cusp of entering into the promised land. Moses has been told that he is not to enter the promised land with them, and so he gives his last words of counsel and advice. Near the end of this powerful book of scripture, in a crucial section, he assures the people: "The word is very near to you; it is in your mouth and in your heart." His teaching is an invitation for God's people to take the words of the law into their hearts and to trust that God has given those words into the care of the people so that they might live out their intimate covenant relationship with God. Some years ago, Martin Smith, then the superior of an Anglican monastic order, the Society of St. John the Evangelist, titled his book on prayerfully reading scripture, *The Word is Very Near You.* The book gently but firmly invites the reader to apply the words and images of scripture to daily life.

The prayer that I offer here replaces the word "word" with the word "work." Here then, taken from Deuteronomy 30:11-20, is Moses' teaching, abbreviated and slightly altered as an invitation to imagine that the work that God would have us do next is close to hand. (The words I changed or added are in italics.)

> Surely the commandment that I am commanding
> you today is not too hard for you, nor is it too far
> away...no, the *work* is very near to you; it is in your
> mouth and in your heart *and in your hands*...I have
> set before you today life and prosperity, death and
> adversity...Choose life that you and your descendants
> may live,loving the LORD your God.

The act of doing the next thing that God would have us do is as life-giving as bearing in our mouths and hearts the words of scripture. The two are intimately connected. The more we know the words of scripture, the more likely we are to understand what good work God would have us do next. To make a start, we pray, especially in times of transition, by simply saying to ourselves, "The work is very near you."

I have found that my times of transition frequently happen in the car and on the stairs. I first introduced this prayer into my daily life on my short commute to work. Getting out of my driveway and through the neighborhood always requires staying alert, so it's usually not until I'm through the first stoplight and onto a road with timed lights that my thoughts settle down, and I remind myself, "The work is very near you." Sometimes I think about my schedule of the day to come, but more often, I attend to the way I drive: being a benevolent driver in the clogged Bay Area is an active challenge. I strive to be both a courteous and non-judgmental driver. If I attend to my breath, I can usually maintain an even temper through my commute. Not judging other drivers with my thoughts is more of a challenge. And yet isn't that what Jesus asks us to do? And what a clear and straightforward place to practice! Bad drivers are all around us, providing multiple opportunities to work on our moral life.

Walking up stairs and saying this occasional prayer gives me an opportunity to think of work in the more concrete sense of the term. My office is upstairs, and the front door of my house has a landing with a few stairs. Here, I often think of the most demanding work or tasks that I sense I'm avoiding and find the determination to do that work first.

Jacob attended a class I taught on this practice. In the week after receiving this teaching, he prayed this prayer after leaving a room. Toward the end of his tenure at a health clinic, he brought in a city official with whom he had a working relationship from a previous position. His only task was to make the initial introduction between the official and two of his younger colleagues at the clinic. They were set to have a difficult conversation about city regulations and the operation of the clinic. The conversation began in a tense and unpleasant way, and Jacob, with his part of the work over, was relieved to offer a light-hearted comment and make his way out the door. Partway down the hall, Jacob thought to himself, "The work is very near you," and he stopped. He listened to his heart, not his head, and realized that his work right now was to stand by his young colleagues, simply as a non-anxious presence, and provide silent moral support. Jacob turned around, entered back into the room with another light-hearted comment, and sat back down. He felt deep assurance afterward that he had done the work God had given him to do.

The post-communion prayer in Rite I in *The Book of Common Prayer* has a sentence that invites an even deeper reflection on this simple practice of reminding ourselves that the work that God would have us do next always lies close to hand. After receiving communion, we pray:

> *And we humbly beseech thee, O heavenly Father,*
> *so to assist us with thy grace, that we may continue*
> *in that holy fellowship, and do all such good works*
> *as thou hast prepared for us to walk in.*[4]

Not only is the emphasis on doing the work, whatever that might be, but also it is explicit that we are to believe that the work has been prepared for us ahead of time. In one of the grandest promises in all scripture, Jesus assures us that he goes ahead of us to prepare a place for us in his Father's house. Jesus tells us, "In my Father's house there are many dwelling places. If it were not so, would I have told you that I go to prepare a place for you? And if I go and prepare a place for you, I will come again and will take you to myself, so that where I am, there you may be also" (John 14:2-3). This passage, often read at funerals, helps us to imagine that the person who has just died is in a room that Jesus prepared just for them. In many small ways through the course of our ordinary days, we are invited to imagine something similar. God goes before each of us, preparing work for us to do. In keeping with the invitation to spiritual growth of this book, the prayer uses the metaphor "all such good works as thou hast prepared for us to *walk* in." If we have well-worn Camino boots of daily prayer and weekly worship, we are much more likely to perceive and do the work God gives us to do. We, like Jacob, are more inclined to turn and do the right thing. As Moses admonishes, we are more likely to choose life and blessing, not death and curses.

As we repeat this occasional prayer to ourselves, what begins to emerge is a consoling intuition of God's governance and providence. As believers, it is probably not difficult to accept the claim of the grand old song, "He's got the whole world in his hands." But if we start to act as though God has prepared good work for us, we begin to shift our understanding of that hand of God. The hand is no longer merely a secure floor under us; it is a shaping hand, always moving before us. Internalizing a sense that God is always moving ahead of us, preparing the next piece of work that we are invited to do, is one of the subtle shifts of the posture of our soul so we may live with gladness and singleness of heart.

To occasionally remind ourselves, "The work is very near you," is an important start to the gentle practices. It is very likely this week that you will wake up one morning and realize that the day before, you didn't think that phrase once. That's okay. Today's a new day. They are called gentle practices because we don't internalize them to improve the posture of our soul through shame. Instead, think of this as a gift that lies close to hand. If you forgot to open the gift yesterday, today is a new day and a new opportunity to say the phrase and see what emerges in your thoughts.

Another word to unpack from this prayer is "send." Each day, we ask God to send us. Or, to put it another way, we remind ourselves that God is sending us. We trust that God is sending us today because we know from scripture that God sends people. One example from the Old Testament is Isaiah, who, in his account of his commissioning as a prophet, writes that he is before the throne of God. "Then I heard the voice of the Lord saying, "Whom shall I send, and who will go for us? And I said, "Here am I; send me!" (Isaiah 6:8). Of course, God immediately makes it clear how difficult the work is that Isaiah is sent to do. He also assures Isaiah that this sending will bear fruit, including the book of Isaiah, which directs and guides Christians in our work today. God sent Isaiah to do work. Isaiah was faithful to that work.

In the New Testament, Jesus repeatedly sends his followers. "Then he said to his disciples, 'The harvest is plentiful, but the laborers are few; therefore ask the Lord of the harvest to send out into his harvest…these twelve [disciples] Jesus sent out with the following instructions…" (Matthew 9:37-38, 10:5). I invite you to embrace and live out your identity as a disciple of Jesus. As we pray each morning, we are following a discipline of our master, Jesus, and so we are his disciples. Disciples of Jesus are sent, not just on special occasions, but each day.

If you are not yet in the custom of praying each day, then I recommend that you bind the saying of this prayer to something you already do every day. For example, you might write out the prayer in your best handwriting and tape it to your bathroom mirror. In my case, even my best efforts might yield something barely legible, but if you have the gift of beautiful writing, make it a text of beauty. At the moment when you put down your toothbrush, say the prayer to God.

Many begin a life of prayer by reading Forward Movement's offering of *Forward Day by Day*. If that is your practice, then simply add the prayer at the end. Another good place to begin daily prayer is by saying the Daily Devotion for Individuals and Families starting on page 137 of *The Book of Common Prayer*. The page includes the portion of a psalm and a few verses of scripture. A simple way to augment the basic structure on the page would be to pray a different psalm each day, beginning with psalm one and then moving to the next psalm each subsequent morning. For another scripture reading, you can choose a book of the Bible such as Philippians, the Gospel of Mark, or Genesis and read a portion each morning. Add the prayer from this chapter as one of the collects. The whole thing need not take more than five minutes.

Ultimately, the goal is to build your way up to twenty minutes a day of prayer. This isn't simply an arbitrary time; research and tradition show that twenty minutes is a good amount of time to settle yourself from other distractions and draw nearer to God.

Two common prayer practices both take about twenty minutes. Centering prayer, a popular kind of Christian meditation taught by Thomas Keating, is twenty minutes for each sit. If you do the full Morning Prayer in *The Book of Common Prayer*, including canticles and the recommended readings and psalms, the process takes twenty minutes. Finally, there is something about our bodies that is linked to about twenty minutes. If we want the full benefits of exercise to change our bodies for a full day, we must exercise for at least between eighteen to twenty minutes.

A key to getting into and maintaining the rhythm of daily prayer is to create a sacred space where you pray each day. For most of us, that means finding a place in our home. I have a desk in an upstairs loft I keep neat and clear. Directly before me is a candle and usually one other object like a cross or a beautiful rock. Close to hand is a Bible, *The Book of Common Prayer*, a journal, and usually some additional spiritual reading. Other people include items such as flowers and incense.

I have one student who cleared out a closet because the lack of stimulation helped her focus. She calls herself a "Closetarian." An acquaintance is the father in a blended family in a small house with lots of children. The only space he can get alone at home is to lock the bathroom door and use the small rug on his floor to cushion his knees and the side of the tub for his elbows as he prays. Another student, who couldn't find the peace at home, leaves early for work, parks each morning beneath a beautiful tree, pulls out an icon from her glove compartment and props it on her windshield. What's most important is the regularity of using a particular space. We gradually train our bodies and minds to be in a place of receptivity when we enter the space. Having a ritual that cues our bodies, such as lighting a candle and taking deep breaths, also helps set the tone for the time of prayer.

The invitation is to pray first thing in the morning. Not only does research show that we are most likely to maintain any practice, such as physical exercise, if we do it first thing in the morning, but also in the case of prayer, it sets the tone for the day. This is particularly important in the coming weeks as you gradually engage the gentle practices. Our prayer time becomes a place where we can both reflect on the previous day and set an intention for the day that is to come. After some experimentation, I found that the daily prayer I introduce at the beginning of this chapter works well for me at the end of a meditation sit. After this time of quiet reflection, I say the words of the prayer slowly and attend to them.

In this first week, whether this is your very first time with a practice of daily prayer or if you are a veteran prayer, I invite you to hold in your imagination an image from the early Christian desert hermits. A great scholar approached one of the hermits, Macarius, and said, "Father, give me a word to live by." Macarius then responded, "Secure the anchor rope to the rock, and by the grace of God, the ship will ride the devilish waves of this beguiling sea."[5]

For this coming week, say each day—and throughout the day—the prayer, "O God, send me this day to do the work you have given me to do, to love and serve you with gladness and singleness of heart." Imagine this prayer is securing your boat to the rock. The prayer itself is the anchor line, and, with your conscious mind, you are deliberately, first thing in the morning, connecting the boat of your heart to Jesus. In a moment, you are going to get up from your prayer chair and fix breakfast. Your work is to begin to trust that, for this day, your heart is anchored in Jesus. You will face difficulties and uncertainties in the day to come. And, especially if you are alert, you will receive gifts and graces. Your mission today is to do the work that is very near you and to be open to the possibility that by doing so, you are loving and serving God. Identifying the gifts of gladness, singleness, and a grateful heart is the work of subsequent weeks. For this week, get in the habit of anchoring your heart to Jesus each morning in prayer and, from time to time, reassuring yourself that, by grace, "The work is very near you."

Finally, remember to be gentle with yourself. This practice, and all the practices of this book, are not tests we need to pass to be seen as good girls and boys by teacher God. There's no deadline for the exam, and there's no grading, even on a curve. These practices are like a series of doorways that we are simply invited to walk through. Particularly the first time you work through this book, some doorways will be more inviting than others. What Abbot Chapman said of prayer, I say of these practices: practice them as you can; and don't try to practice them as you can't. Sometimes a gentle practice at first seems awkward, but it will, over the course of the week, slowly reveal its sense to you. Other times, a practice may never quite fit. The first time I taught this process, five people completed the series. When I asked a few weeks after the teaching which of the gentle practices had stayed with us, we were evenly distributed.

You have an adventure of spiritual discovery before you. By engaging each of the gentle practices, you will discover your soul and improve its posture. But before you begin your first gentle practice, you must prepare your heart with daily prayer. So, write or type out the prayer and put it in the space where you intend to pray for the next week. Then, ever so gently and from time to time, particularly in moments of transition, remind yourself: "The work is very near you."

THIS WEEK

The Work Is Very Near You.

SHIFT

Identify as your call whatever work
God would have you do next.

REPETITION

Choose three daily times of transition in
your ordinary day and, this week,
say to yourself, "The work is very near you,"
each time you are in that place
and time of transition.

CAMINO BOOTS

Commit to weekly worship
and twenty minutes of prayer.

CHAPTER TWO
Look at Each Face

GENTLE PRACTICE

Look at each face and remember
that they are a PERSON

WORDS

Gladness   PERSON
Theotropic   Enigma

*O God, send me this day to do the work
you have given me to do, to love and serve you
with gladness and singleness of heart.* Amen.

Look at Each Face

Nothing is more fascinating than a human face. One of the great pleasures of going to a great museum is the opportunity to stare as long as you want at a human face in a great portrait painting. Paintings by masters such as Rembrandt or Diego Velázquez seem to capture all the subtlety, ambiguity, and emotional shading of a real face. It is no mistake that the world's most famous painting, the *Mona Lisa*, is of an elusive and compelling human face. Even so, not one face painted by any of these masters is greater than the human faces you will see in the coming week. The first gentle practice invites us to look at each face with the reverence due to one made in the image and likeness of God.

This gentle practice invites us to remember the word "gladness." The source of our liturgical phrase, "with gladness and singleness of heart," is a passage from the book of Acts that describes the ideal beginning of the church. Through the centuries, many have used these descriptions of church in the second chapter of Acts as a motivator to be a thriving and holy church in different times and places. In chapter two of Acts, we are told that the disciples gathered together and broke bread "with glad and generous hearts" (Acts 2:46). The word gladness expresses a kind of joyful conviviality, evoking lively and deep gratitude for the gift of being human together, of knowing that we are brothers and sisters in Christ as we share life together. Our outward unity in Christ makes explicit a deep truth that our unity is not only all people but also with all creation. The Gospel of John tells us that "all things came into being through him, and without him not one thing came into being" (John 1:3). In Christ, all are one, all of creation. This unity includes each human face we see, and so each face has the potential, when we remember this deep truth, to bring gladness.

Looking at each face makes use of our eyes. The spiritual life is filled with visual images. When God creates the world in Genesis, we are told that God "sees" everything that is made and that it is "very good" (Genesis 1:31). Two of the most moving stories in the gospel involve sight. In a story found only in the Gospel of Mark, Jesus partially heals a man. He tells Jesus, "I can see people, but they look like trees, walking" (Mark 8:24). Jesus lays hands on him again, and the man's sight is fully restored. In John, an entire chapter is dedicated to the healing of the man born blind, who at one point famously decrees, "I do not know whether [Jesus] is a sinner. One thing I do know, that though I was blind, now I see" (John 9:25). These stories invite us to imagine both the bestowing of visual sight and the gift of spiritual sight. The story in the Gospel of John inspired the line, "I once was blind, but now I see," in "Amazing Grace." Englishman John Newton was a slave trader who became an abolitionist after his conversion to Christianity. I imagine that he wrote the song when he realized that the people in his boat were not commodities but people, and so he recognized that each one was made in the image and likeness of God.

As we move through the coming week, we will encounter three kinds of faces: planned, unplanned, and anonymous. A first step is to simply be alert to which type of face is before your eyes. A planned face is a known face. As I write this, I am sheltering in place with my family, which I have been doing for two months. I always wake up first, followed by my wife, who gets her coffee before her prayers, then my younger son, who gets a bowl of cereal before going downstairs for virtual high school, and then my older son, who gets up last of all to make a smoothie before a virtual college class. I have a view of these planned faces from my home desk. As I move into my gentle practice of looking at each face, I ask myself: Can I look at these faces in a fresh way, or am I in a rut? Can I remember each day that this face, known well to me, was made in the image and likeness of God? Am I in a rut with how I view this face, in my relationship and in how I see the face of Christ in this familiar person?

The second kind of face is unplanned. When I first taught this material, I made my way to a meeting at church. I arrived about ten minutes early so that I could be there to welcome the known and loved faces of Jacob, Judy, Tanner, Michael, Joan, and Kate. As I pulled into the parking lot, I saw Samantha sitting on an outdoor bench, waiting for me. I got out of the car and sat down next to her. She and I had been texting earlier in the week because she had some things she wanted to tell me, and she needed my help. Samantha was part of a support group for teen mothers I had helped facilitate. Samantha explained that her phone had died, and she didn't have the means to fix it or get a new one. She then began to speak and cry, and I settled in for what I knew would be a long time with Samantha.

I am confident that, even before arriving at the teaching in this chapter, I would have chosen to stay with Samantha, at least for a time. But now that I was embracing the gentle practice of looking at each face, I was more aware of the mystery that unplanned faces during my day may not be part of my plan but were probably part of God's. I settled fully into being with Samantha, my heart undivided, allowing her to set the time. I was late for my other meeting, but the work of the day was very near me, in the face of Samantha. Our time together was a piece of the good work God had prepared for me to walk in that week. When we encounter unplanned or expected faces, are we alert and responsive? Do we set aside our own timelines and to-do's and focus on the person in front of us?

When I was able to join my planned meeting, I found they had (as I had hoped) started without me. When I briefly explained why I was late, they could not have been more gracious. It was easy to look on their faces with gladness. Yet my time with Samantha, though unexpected, had tapped into an even deeper sort of gladness. Jesus has a special love for those of us who are broken, poor, or on the margins. When we are invited to intimately love those whom Jesus especially loves, it is a taste of the gladness of the gospel.

The third kind of face can be the most difficult. We experience two types of challenges with anonymous faces, those of people we don't know. The first is the way we tend to project onto people. It is far too easy to look at people and have our lust, envy, or judgment triggered. Our primal emotions, if we are putting words to them on our minds, frequently create thoughts we wouldn't want to say out loud: "What a nice butt!" or "I wish I had hair like that!" or "What was he thinking with that shirt?" The habit of these unholy thoughts is, I suspect, a sin that plagues all of us. When we go into places with crowds, before we start gazing at faces, it's important to remind ourselves how easily our fellow human beings can trigger uncharitable thoughts. We need to attend to our thoughts, such that we become aware when our mind begins to teem with dehumanizing observations of our brothers and sisters.

We may need to hit the reset button. This often means practicing stewardship of the eyes, looking down at the ground and negotiating our way through the space without the temptation to judge others. It can be particularly helpful at this time to say to ourselves the Lord's Prayer, a few Hail Marys, the Jesus Prayer ("Lord Jesus Christ, son of the living God, have mercy on me, a sinner."), or a favorite piece of scripture. After a time, we may then be ready to look on our fellow human beings with gratitude, not judgment.

Twentieth-century philosopher Ludwig Wittgenstien wrote, "The face is the soul of the body." He reflects here a truth that the face is the fullest possible image on earth of our soul. Because this is so, and because our souls, by God's grace, can be eternal, what we look at in a human face is a shimmering of eternity in time. Our work as followers of Christ is to look at each human face as a PERSON. The word is purposefully written in all capital letters. Many translations of the Bible, including the New Revised Standard Version, show reverence for God by always covering the letters that refer to God's name with an all capital letters version of the word "lord." The letters JHWH refer to God's words to Moses from the burning bush.

Some choose to say the letters aloud as one of two names, either Jahweh or Jehovah. Following the lead of the NRSV and as a practice of reverence for God, I choose not to say those names of God aloud but know they are there when I see the word LORD. It is one way to honor the divinity of God.

Similarly, I encourage us to honor Christ in each PERSON we encounter. As part of the gentle practice of looking at each face, I repeat to myself two words that remind me of the PERSON's holiness. The first word is "theotropic," a real word even though my computer doesn't recognize it! Sunflowers are heliotropic. This means that the surface of the flower always tilts toward the place in the sky where it will receive the most sun. This is why, when you go past a field of sunflowers, they are tilting in the same direction. They are doing the thing that God created them to do. In a way similar to sunflowers and the sun, God created us to tilt toward God.

We were made in the image and likeness of God, each human being, with no exceptions. No matter how ugly, depressed, distracted, depraved, angry, judgmental, or mendacious a person appears to us, they are theotropic, created to tilt toward God like sunflowers tilt to the sun. Remembering this word, and believing it to be true of each face, shifts us.

The second word is enigma. I once read a review of a movie with one of my favorite actors. This actor is one of a handful of people who will motivate me to see a movie, even if I'm not convinced by the plot description. In this movie, she played a Russian spy with secrets. The reviewer said the film failed because, regardless of this actor's formidable gifts, the character came across as a "cipher" and not an "enigma." A cipher is one on whom we project a flimsy and disposable set of assumptions. They appear as a shallow paste-up job out of our imaginations and our desires. An enigma, on the other hand, is a compelling mystery. The character-driven movies we return to repeatedly are filled with characters who are enigmatic. The actors have persuasively inhabited the lives of full human beings, with all of our contradictions, evasions, and depths.

This week's gentle practice is to look at each face and remember that the human face before us in any given moment is the face of a PERSON who is a theotropic enigma. Together, these words remind us that the person before us, whether a best friend or a stranger, is both known by us and unknown by us. As a person of faith who believes with scripture that we are each made in the image and likeness of God, we can also believe that the person before us is made in the image and likeness of God and desires to be one with God. This is true of us from the moment of our conception to, God willing, our partaking of eternal life at the heavenly banquet. Remembering this deep reality can be particularly powerful when we encounter someone who is mean, angry, or unpleasant. We know they have a desire for God within them, and we also humbly acknowledge that there is much we don't and cannot know. The person before us is a mystery to us, whose thoughts, joys, sufferings, vices, and virtues are known fully only to God. The practice is to refrain from claiming to know more than we possibly could of the human being before us.

Tanner found a way to perform this daily practice. He takes the bus into the city for his work as an insurance agent. The bus has tinted windows, allowing him to look out at people without being seen in return. As part of his spiritual practice, Tanner looks at the faces of the people on the street and remembers the words that I have shared with you. He sees each PERSON as a theotropic enigma. By consciously naming the face of each person, he recognizes that they are made in the image of God, full of holy mystery.

One way we love God is to give the honor due God's name. We sing and pray the Name above all names and refer to the Source of all being, an incomprehensible mystery in whom we live and move and have our being. When it comes to God, we now see through a glass darkly, but in the age to come, we will, according to reliable Paul of Tarsus, see God face to face (1 Corinthians 13:12). We now see other human beings face to face. We don't have to wait for the life to be revealed to each of us after our death to see the faces of our family, friends, brothers, and sisters in Christ and the anonymous crowd. Those faces are there for us to gaze upon with wonder and gratitude. It is True with a capital "T" that each human being was made in the image and likeness of God, and so is, like you, a theotropic enigma. This week, look at each face and remember that each is a PERSON. See if remembering this truth makes your heart glad.

THIS WEEK

Look at each face and remember
that they are a PERSON.

SHIFT

Practice stewardship of your eyes,
particularly around people.

REPETITION

Each day, attend to the faces you see regularly,
such as family, friends, and co-workers,
and remember that each one is a PERSON.

CAMINO BOOTS

Commit to weekly worship and
twenty minutes of prayer.

CHAPTER THREE
Name Each Work

GENTLE PRACTICE

Name each work and so learn to
mindfully do one thing at a time.

WORDS

Singleness   Repetition

Conviction

*O God, send me this day to do the work
you have given me to do, to love and serve you
with gladness and singleness of heart.* Amen.

Name Each Work

The word "singleness" animates this week's gentle practice.
The practice builds on the occasional reminder we learned in
the first week, where, in times of transition, we say to ourselves,
"The work is very near you." Notice that what is near to us is
not plural; it is work and not "works." In the coming week,
there will be lots of discrete pieces of work that become plural.
This week, however, our practice is to look for the single, next
piece of work. This practice consists of getting into the habit
of naming the work that we are about to do or are in the act of
doing. The act of naming slows us down, clarifies our focus,
and increases our intentionality. The ultimate goal of this week
is purity and wholeness of heart.

God, from the very beginning, gave human beings the authority
to use words. In our creative work of naming, we can, like
Adam, be co-creators with God. Our creation story tells us "out
of the ground the Lord God formed every animal of the field
and every bird of the air, and brought them to the man to see
what he would call them; and whatever the man called every
living creature, that was its name" (Genesis 2:19). The work
of naming lions, tigers, and bears has already been done. The
work of naming our next work lies before us, and there is no
one in the world but ourselves who can do the creative work
of naming the next single piece of work that we are just about
to do. The deep connection between words and works is at the
source of poetry. The etymology for the word poet is Greek
for maker, from *poiein*, which means to create. The Christian

poet W.H. Auden has a fine portion of a poem called "The Cave of Making" that he dedicates to a fellow poet, whom he calls a "maker."[6] In the poem, Auden claims priority for their shared craft of shaping words into poems over the plastic art of painting. Their art of carefully shaping words is an art we can share each day. By becoming deliberate in our use of words, we can become like poets of our days, stringing words together in sequence in such a way that our days have form and beauty.

Words have the power to alter reality. Coleridge's words at the beginning of his *Aids to Reflection* take on even greater importance as we begin intentionally naming each work that is before us. He wrote, "accustom yourself to reflect on the words you use... for if words are not things, they are living powers, by which things of most importance to (humankind) are actuated, combined and humanized."[7] As Christians, it ought to be no great leap to believe with Coleridge that words are "living powers." Scripture for us is like a savannah teeming with living words. As Christians, we have the custom, when quoting Jesus, of not writing "Jesus said...", which we would write of any other historical figure, but rather "Jesus says...." For example, we might say, "Jesus says, 'Come to me all ye that are weary and carrying heavy burdens, and I will give you rest'" (Matthew 11:28). We put Jesus' words in the present tense because the invitation still stands in this moment, right now, and it stands, as Hebrews has it, "yesterday and today and forever" (Hebrews 13:8). We say, in the congregational response in Eucharistic Prayer A, "Christ has died, Christ is risen, Christ will come again" (*The Book of Common Prayer*, p. 363). His words in scripture are still living powers.

Further, as people of both word and sacrament, it is words as living powers that give us the assurance that this water, in this bowl, becomes the water of baptism, and so enables us to welcome this infant, child, youth, or adult into the household of Christ. Likewise, it is words as living powers that give us the assurance that this bread and wine really become the body and blood of Jesus for us in the moment the words are spoken, the gestures made, the bread broken, and the wine poured out. These primal gestures, with words, don't take place apart from reality. Rather, they ground all of our reality in the truth of the real God. Our words matter because in our scriptures, our sacraments, and our daily lives, they are living powers.

Coleridge specifies that living words actuate, combine, and humanize. One of the most fraught encounters I have is when people park in the small lot of our church to use a local business or worship at a neighboring church. Three times in the last six months, I have, with my clerical collar on, asked someone to leave because the parking lot was for St. Paul's only. All three times, I have been met with unhinged rage and accusations of how angry I am, which I'm not, and insults that I am a terrible priest and no kind of Christian. As I receive and deflect the invective internally, I say to myself, "I am holding a boundary for my sheep." For years, I was unable to hold that boundary for fear of the anger I knew would come my way. I use my words, like an obedient preschooler, to have a more healthy relationship with my emotions, and so a more healthy response to the conflicts I encounter in the world. In my defense of St. Paul's small parking lot, claiming the word "boundary" had dramatic results that actuated a new norm. For years, I would frequently avoid the confrontations with the trespassers. When I did engage with them, I would often either give permission and tell them "never again" or occasionally gird myself up for the confrontation by getting angry. The word boundary made actual the gift of calm authority in me.

That same word also combines several external realities. The vestry worked very hard to create a lot that was laid out for ease of use with plenty of signage so that people knew where they were to park and whether they were allowed to park there. This included a big sign, with our logo, using the precise language the town requires to give us the authority to ticket and tow. The preschool on our campus has specific needs, particularly in times of drop-off and pick up. As I held the boundary, I combined the hopes and intentions of all those leaders.

Finally, my new stance in the face of the rage and the shame of the trespassers is a harmonization of thoughts in me, the fruit of years of prayer practice. As I stand calmly and listen to the rant, feelings of anger, uncertainty, fear, discomfort, and a bit of shame all make an effort to elbow their way into my consciousness. After all, the trespassers are using the living power of words too. But years of Christian meditation have taught me to gently let go of afflictive thoughts and emotions, to feel the feeling, and return to the center. Thanks to a daily prayer practice, the discordant attacks of the trespassers now fail to ruin the harmonious and simple response of holding a firm and appropriate boundary.

I pull into our small parking lot multiple times a week and am always alert to the cars that are in it. I rarely need to hold the boundary in such a dramatic fashion. Every day gives an opportunity to use less emotionally fraught words to gradually order our ordinary days. The movie *Groundhog Day* reveals, under extraordinary circumstances, the profound truth that our lives are filled with repetitions. Bill Murray plays a jaded TV weatherman on his annual assignment to cover Groundhog Day in the small town of Punxsutawney. He becomes stuck in a time loop where, every morning, he wakes up midway through the song "I Got You Babe" on the clock radio and then proceeds to have the same encounters with the same people in the same places day after day, in a seemingly endless series of repetitions. He soon discovers that he can alter the encounters in ways that amuse him. At first, he takes the repetitions in a dark direction, mocking the foolishness of the others. After a time, he begins to go in the opposite direction, gradually becoming more kind, using his foreknowledge to do good.

Our daily lives are filled with repetitions, more similar to the experience of Bill Murray's character than we are likely to admit. Retired Admiral William H. McRaven turned a graduation speech into a bestseller called *Make Your Bed: Little Things That Can Change Your Life… And Maybe the World*. It is a series of ten pieces of life advice, the first of which is to make your bed well each morning, a discipline McRaven learned as a Navy SEAL. In his training for that elite corps, he writes that passing bed inspection "demonstrated my discipline. It showed my attention to detail, and at the end of the day, it would be a reminder that I had done something well, something to be proud of, no matter how small the task."[8] The repetition of making the bed is a repetition that grounds the day and sets the tone for what is to come. In a similar spirit, my current challenge in naming work and nurturing singleness of heart is preparing breakfast. As I applied this week's gentle practice of naming each work, I noticed that my breakfast ritual had a peculiar and unnecessary intensity. Some old and now inaccurate tape in my head had me needing to rush out the door, and so the tasks of toasting bread, eating a banana, preparing cereal, and checking on the daily news on (I kid you not!) ten different websites all somehow had to take place simultaneously. I was not setting myself up to live "with gladness and singleness of heart" in the coming day.

With the use of words, I am slowly disentangling this needless knot and attempting to do one thing at a time. Here, the fact that my breakfast routine is a lot like *Groundhog Day* is an advantage. It is easy to notice when I am mindful and deliberate—and when I'm back to tackling breakfast like an ER professional, as though someone's life depends on the speed in which I eat my cereal. This first encounter with the day's worldly tasks, like McRaven's bed-making, sets a tone for the day. It is also an excellent way to embrace this action as a truly gentle practice. I fail nearly every day in my attempt at mindful breakfast making. I also am making gradual progress. I hope it is like the practice of learning a scale on an instrument. One fumbles many times before the fingers finally traverse the scale with confidence. And even then, one must return to the scale each day to keep the muscle memory strong and clear.

This gentle practice of naming ordinary work and becoming alert to it has its Christian roots in the Rule of Saint Benedict. He writes that the monastery cellarer, the one who takes care of the common goods, is to "regard all utensils and goods of the monastery as sacred vessels of the altar, aware that nothing is to be neglected."[9]

Although Brigitte was initially one of my students in these gentle practices, she has become my teacher in naming each work. When we began to shelter in place in response to COVID-19, Brigitte wanted to approach the restriction as an invitation to a spiritual retreat. One of the foundations of her retreat in place was to fully embrace this practice of naming each work and doing each task discretely and well. At first, she wanted to be predominately in silence. Finally, after some weeks, we checked in, and she reported that her experience of slowing down and paying attention had been transformative.

She is in her eighties and beginning to struggle with her balance. She found that this simple practice gave her much more confidence in, for example, negotiating the stairs. She named the task of walking each step, breaking the obstacle into smaller pieces that she had confidence in accomplishing. By rooting the simple daily task of walking up and down stairs safely in her spiritual practice, she gradually lost her fear of falling. Having infused a simple daily challenge with fresh intentionality, Brigitte then returned to the more complex task of creating her visual art of painting and collage. In her art, the new practice of naming work opened a vein of creativity and inspiration. As I thought about Brigitte and her embrace of this gentle practice, first with her stairs and then with her art, I was reminded how she leads public scripture readings in church. She is one of those readers who you follow with great attention and pleasure because she is slow and deliberate; she manages to make the scripture passages sound as though she is discovering each word at the same time as you, her listener.

Naming each work is a mundane, everyday practice that opens us to the profound possibility of purity of heart. Jesus teaches, "Blessed are the pure in heart, for they will see God" (Matthew 5:8). Building on his master's teaching, James admonishes fellow followers of Jesus to "draw near to God and he will draw near to you...purify your hearts, you double-minded" (James 4:8). The book of James was the favorite New Testament book of Christian theologian and poet Søren Kierkegaard. In "Purity of Heart Is to Will One Thing," one of many essays inspired by the words of James's Epistle, Kierkegaard demonstrates the wide range of ways we human beings are capable of being double-minded and so fail, in the language of this week's gentle practice, in not having singleness of heart. Kierkegaard is a master of surfacing the wily ways of the human heart and mind before the infinite and eternal mystery of God. For this week, the most useful style of our double-mindedness is what Kierkegaard identifies as "busyness."

It is tough for us not to be or appear busy. If we slow down and do one thing at a time, the words that are likely to come to mind are negative. In English, almost all of the antonyms for busyness are things we are taught to avoid. These antonyms include lazy, indolent, inactive, idle, and lackadaisical. It also includes a bunch of words with "un" for a prefix: unoccupied, unengaged, and uninterested. None of these are words we would want a teacher or a boss writing about us in a letter of recommendation. They are the sorts of self-accusatory words that may emerge when we pursue only one work at a time rather than the seemingly more productive technique of multitasking. When we slow down and increase intentionality, we are likely to feel not busy enough.

Kierkegaard observes that the push for busyness brings with it a terrible cost. He claims that in our busyness, "there is neither the time nor the tranquility to acquire a conviction. That is why in life's busyness even faith, hope, and love and willing the good become nothing but flabby words and double-mindedness."[10] This coming week, as we practice naming our work and strive for singleness, we will be fighting *against* the temptation to allow others or ourselves to call us lazy. We will be fighting *for* conviction. The work of each week is aimed toward giving us a single conviction. Our goal is to shift from being primarily a disciple of Jesus, that is, one who practices the disciplines he taught, to being a pilgrim, that is, one who is on the way, with Jesus, toward our spiritual home. Our busyness is one of the tenacious ways we keep ourselves from the conviction that we are God's child, and we are on our way home.

This gentle practice produced a profound and surprising shift in me. Over some months, I had gradually been trying this gentle practice more frequently, often saying to myself simple things like "I am driving courteously" or "I am doing the dishes." Perhaps I was a little more focused than before, but I wasn't sure. As is often the case with spiritual practices, the fruit of it wasn't immediately apparent. Then my younger son and I left for a weeklong tour of colleges. The trip involved six airports, transportation by both Uber and rental car, and, on most days, scheduled visits to two college campuses. For me, the week was laid out like an emotional minefield. Generally, just walking into an airport kicks my anxiety up to a high level. My head becomes filled with all the possible bad outcomes from being robbed to missing the plane. The two cities where we visited schools were like an extension of the airport, with each visit requiring multiple decisions and a strict timeline. To have my younger son, who is like me in temperament, by my side, was like having my judgmental thoughts spoken aloud but at great public volume. All this emotional turmoil was what I had anticipated.

The reality of my experience throughout the week was just the opposite. As I left the parking garage shuttle, I kept up a simple narrative in my head. "I am walking across the street." "I am getting my ticket from the machine." "I am waiting in line." I didn't check my phone, nor did I think more than one move in advance. I simply focused on the thing that was before me. I was remarkably attentive to my son. His anxious questioning, even when he was correct in his concerns, didn't ruffle my calm. This strange peace continued throughout the week of college visits. At one point, we were driving from one college to another, the timing was tight, and my son, for understandable reasons, had misread the instructions on the GPS. We were headed the wrong way, uncertain of our ability to turn around any time soon. Six months before, my breathing would have been shallow, my thoughts catastrophic, and my fuse short. I would certainly have snapped at my son. Mysteriously to me, I was calm and felt compassion for my son. At the moment, I knew that the work that was near me was graciously figuring a way out of this dilemma with my son. Being calm and gracious in the moment was the work I was to do with singleness, not the work of arriving on time for a college tour.

As we move through the book, you will find that each of the gentle practices corresponds to a place in our bodies. For instance, look at each face asks us to attend to our eyes. Name your work is both more abstract and often the most concrete. It asks us to attend to what is going on between our ears, that is, in our minds. We are to assess the quality of the words we use and their fittingness for the work before us. These words can be placed on a scale from the concrete to the abstract. Start with the simple words that describe the task before you: crossing the street, waiting in line, and doing the dishes. These are the most kinesthetic. We can observe our hands buttering the toast. We might then discover words that combine describing an action with certain qualities of how the action is performed. For instance, holding a boundary not only described my request that a trespasser not park in the St. Paul's lot, but it also evoked a certain quality of authority and the way in which I stand for two communities, the church and the preschool. The word boundary, which took me years to discover, is thick with meaning when I stand beside my car and politely ask someone to leave.

There is another level of abstraction when we use a word to qualify the way we would like to go about doing a particular work. As an example, it is my goal to drive courteously. Over the years, I have refined a list of virtues that I am drawn to nurture in myself, by God's grace. Courtesy is one of them. One of the reasons Julian of Norwich's *Revelations* are so stirring to me and to many is the beautiful and loving courtesy she describes in the relationship she has with her Lord Jesus.

I often wonder what it would be like if I consistently drove my car with the attentiveness, kindness, generosity, patience, and, most difficult of all, the non-judgmental pity that the word "courteous" can mean in its full flowering. The word courteous comes from the word "court," as in the court of the queen, and in a medieval context, courtesy would have meant a very specific code of behavior. If one were of the aristocracy, one would have been trained from a young age in the particular behavior the court required. These behaviors would range from manners of address according to rank to how one was to dress and eat.

Our manners are much looser, which gives a broader range to what can be considered courteous or not. In the twenty-first century, we are left with the more nebulous and negotiable bare standard of "Do to others as you would have them do to you" (Luke 6:31). My goal is to drive such that, if all drove like me, driving would be a more graceful and peaceful experience. Like preparing breakfast sequentially, I have the opportunity every day to exercise courtesy while I drive. Like my breakfast practice, it is humbling how often I fall short. But I fall, and I get up again, I fall down, and I get up again.

In his essay on purity of heart, Kierkegaard names four virtues that diminish when we are consumed with busyness. These are "faith, hope, love, and willing the good."[11] Busyness chokes out our conviction that virtues are worth pursuing and embodying. Willing the good and these three theological virtues are all higher in the hierarchy of virtues than courtesy. They are the most important virtues for any Christian. Part of the fruit of this practice of doing one work at a time and then using our words to name that work is that busyness decreases, and our conviction increases. A decrease in busyness and an increase of conviction leaves space for serenity. Serenity increases our receptivity to the good gifts of faith, hope, and love. In a pivotal passage in the essay, Kierkegaard compares a serene heart to a deep ocean, an image to carry in our minds this week as we name each work:

> Just as the ocean, when it lies still this way, deeply transparent, aspires to heaven, so the pure heart, when it is still, deeply transparent, aspires solely to the good; or just as the ocean becomes pure when it aspires only to heaven, so the heart becomes pure when it aspires only to the good. Just as the ocean reflects the height of heaven in its pure depth, so the heart, when it is still and deeply transparent, reflects in its pure depth the heavenly sublimity of the good.[12]

THIS WEEK

Name each work and so learn to
mindfully do one thing at a time.

SHIFT

Release the temptation to multitask.

REPETITION

Choose an activity you do every day,
like making breakfast,
and name each distinct action.

CAMINO BOOTS

Commit to weekly worship and
twenty minutes of prayer.

CHAPTER FOUR

Pray and Reflect
on the Sabbath

GENTLE PRACTICE

On Sunday, before worship,
say the sabbath prayer and then reflect
on the last week and the week to come.

WORDS

Reflection	Source	Light
House	Mirror	Vineyard
	Sabbath	

SABBATH PRAYER

O God, in your light we see light;
help me reflect on the week that has passed,
that I may remember in truth, and on the week to come,
that I may be ready to do all such good works
as thou hast prepared for me to walk in,
in the name of Jesus, the light of the world. Amen.

Pray and Reflect on the Sabbath

A good coach knows how hard to push her athletes and when to give them rest. Without a day of rest or of very light exercise, the body tends to burn itself out. The pause and the rest are part of gradually building up strength and flexibility in our bodies. It is in this training spirit that we approach the sabbath with our souls. We have, over the last few weeks, added a daily prayer and three gentle practices. We are saying to ourselves throughout the day, "The work is very near you." As we look at a human face, we remind ourselves that the one we are looking at is a PERSON. And we are finding words for the things we are doing in our daily lives, perhaps identifying tasks like making the bed, preparing breakfast, or driving to regular appointments, and seeing what happens as we name each work. In particular, we look to the act of naming as a way to decrease our busyness so that we may pursue a single work at a time rather than juggling many works at once. These gentle practices are our exercises, and we do them in the hopes that they will gradually improve the posture of our soul. This week's practice, to pray and reflect on the sabbath, is an opportunity to consolidate what we have learned so far and prepare our souls for the next three gentle practices.

This Sunday, we are to find a place and a time of quiet, say a brief prayer, and then spend five to ten minutes remembering the week that has passed and looking forward to the week that is to come.

The prayer is:

> *O God, in your light we see light,*
> *Help me reflect*
> *On the week that has passed that I may remember*
> *in truth, and on the week to come that I may be ready*
> *to do all such good works as thou hast prepared*
> *for me to walk in,*
> *In the name of Jesus, the light of the world.* Amen.

It is well worth putting in some extra effort to memorize the prayer. The prayer both gives the agenda for the time of reflection and wraps it in scripture. The first line, "O God in your light we see light," echoes Psalm 36:9, while the final words come from John 8:12.

Let us begin with memorizing the prayer so that we may inwardly digest it. Poet and theologian Samuel Taylor Coleridge inspired both the prayer and my reflections on it. In his theological work, *Aids to Reflection*, Coleridge encourages us as Christians to claim the word "enlightenment" as our own. We tend to think of the word as describing either a Buddhist state of being or a particular fusion of science, art, and constitutional democracy that emerged in eighteenth-century Europe and America. Coleridge was both a child of the Enlightenment and a leader of Romanticism as well as a faithful practicing Christian. He is a witness to us for how to be enlightened Christians when times are strange and unsettling. We begin the prayer with Coleridge's guiding metaphor of light.

O God, in your light we see light

In our ten minutes of weekly reflection, we are invited to reflect the light of God onto our memories as we look at the past week and onto our imaginations as we look toward the week to come.

Imagine a large clay jar in a garden. The jar is filled with water, and inside the jar is a fountain. The surface of the water is flat except for the very center of the jar. There, the water from the internal fountain looks like marble, with fresh water spilling over the lip of the jar. Now imagine that the sun is setting, and for a moment, as you gaze on the marble of water, it is filled with the bright light of the sun. You witness both source and light.

Coleridge believed that nature spoke to us. Poet Malcolm Guite, a devotee of Coleridge's, believes that the second half of Coleridge's life was spent reflecting on "language considered as a set of symbols given and articulated by humanity and nature considered as a set of symbols given and articulated by God."[13] He imagines that God created nature like a book of life that we can read if we have the eyes to see. Coleridge was headed in this direction even earlier in his life. In an early poem, "Fears in Solitude," Coleridge portrays a humble person listening to a lark, seeing the sun, feeling the breezy air, and responding: "with many feelings, many thoughts, made up a meditative joy, and found religious meanings in the forms of nature!"[14]

The interaction of light and water particularly moved Coleridge. In a notebook, he writes of a "quiet stream, with all its eddies, and the moonlight playing in them, quiet as if they were ideas in the divine mind [before] the Creation."[15]

Coleridge would have called our marble of water in the setting sun a "fontal light," a favorite image he frequently used for the achievement of a good person and for the church itself. I invite us to see this image as an accessible emblem of God as both source and light. We cannot safely stare at our earthly source of light. We stare at the moon, of course, but we know that the moon's light is only a reflection of the light of the sun. To stare at the sun is to go blind. So if we cannot stare at the real source of light, we can at least imagine gazing on this light-filled font.

God is the source of all, so I sometimes allow my mind to reflect on water sources greater than a garden fountain. I love rivers, and one of my favorites is the Sorgue in southern France. It cuts through the center of a town called L'Isle-sur-la-Sorgue in the middle of a plain that hosts an antique market every Sunday. The brass and copper handles on our kitchen cabinets are from a nineteenth-century apothecary and were purchased by my wife from a street vendor there. Several miles upstream from the town, you can rent a kayak for the afternoon and follow the stone banks that once belonged to mills and then travel along the meandering river as it moves through forests and alongside campgrounds. Still further upstream, you can park at a village, right at the foot of the hills, where the poet Petrarch once lived. It was in that village that he saw the lovely and inaccessible Laura. In his pining for her, he wrote hundreds of poems and, in the process, invented the poetic form of the sonnet. If you go past the village, you soon find yourself walking along rocky rapids whose level of agitation varies according to the season. After about half an hour of walking, you arrive at the Fountain de Vaucluse, which is the source of the Sorgue river. In the summer, it is like a blue-green pond, feeding the river from underneath its placid surface. In the spring, water pours out over its rocky lip.

No one has ever been to the bottom of the Fountain de Vaucluse. The famous French sea explorer Jacques Cousteau tried twice, as have others since. It has been determined that only a robot could go the required depth, but that has yet to be attempted. Those who have explored the fountain have discovered ancient coins lodged deep down in the fountain. They believe that the ancient tribes that lived in the area revered the fountain as a place of the gods and the coins were primitive offerings. Light hits this fountain too, and the water that emerges from this fountain is even more generative of natural and human life, delight and industry. How much more is that true of God, the true fontal light?

Help me reflect

The words of the next line of the prayer capture the power of light reflected from God and the freedom and the limitations we have in wielding that light. As we explore this idea of reflection, imagine a mirror, maybe a compact one kept in a purse or bedside table. The mirror offers a way to look at ourselves, but, when held just so, can reflect sunlight out into the room.

The Oxford English Dictionary defines reflection as "the throwing back by a body or surface light, heat, or sound without absorbing it." In our prayer and practice, the time of reflection is not for self-absorbed evaluation. We aren't to revel and repeat stories about ourselves. Rather, the reflection is to be a disciplined chronological remembering of the past week's events and the probable events of the week to come. It is an orderly sweep from one point in time to another, like the beam of a lighthouse.

A second component is that we have freedom of movement—up to a point. Coleridge writes: "A reflecting mind is not a flower that grows wild or comes of its own accord."[16] Rather, we must cultivate a state of reflection and contemplation. Our weekly sabbath reflection gives us a particular freedom of time for reflection so that we may survey past and future events in the light of God, not in the spirit of self-absorption. We give thanks for the moments when our gentle practices yielded moments of grace, ask forgiveness for those times when our hearts were hard, and press on with our sweeping survey.

Reflective thought is also creative thought. In a late lecture, after Coleridge had written most of his brilliant poems, he shared that art begins where there is a "congruity of the animal impression with the reflective powers of the mind."[17] Reflection is the creative art of taking the raw materials of our life as we actually live it and then mindfully and in the light of Christ, shaping a more beautiful life. We have begun to experience this creativity as we name each work we do, and perhaps by doing this naming, we create little poems out of the passing of our ordinary days. For example, if I were able to hold a firm boundary with a rude trespasser on the St. Paul's parking lot and then get into my car and drive all the way home with non-judgmental courtesy, then I would consider such a sequence of events akin to a finely shaped line of a poem.

Now, with this deliberate weekly reflection, we are shaping, in the light of Christ, a new narrative out of our whole lives. In the time of reflection, we remember the work that is near us, the faces we've seen, and the work we've named.

The next section of the prayer invites us to slow down and savor the richness of our memories and the anticipation of the week to come.

On the week that has passed that I may remember in truth, and on the week to come that I may be ready to do all such good works as thou hast prepared for me to walk in

Because we are setting aside ten minutes to remember and anticipate, we can slow down and savor the richness and complexity of what we have experienced and what is likely to come our way in the near future. My wife's family has a house that I have visited every other year for over thirty years. It is in a secluded place in a windy valley. Not only is it alarmed for security, but also the windows and doors have wooden shutters that block out all wind and light. One of life's rich gifts is walking through the house when we first arrive. As I walk through the house and open the shutters to let in light, I feel a flood of memories and a surge of eager anticipation. I see the dining table where we ate lamb feasts with Chloe's now-deceased grandparents, uncles, and aunts. The memories evoke joy, grief, and gratitude. I see the desk where I wrote poems and remember the satisfactions and frustrations of crafting them.

I see the couch where our son, now nineteen, had a febrile seizure at eighteen months and had to be rushed to the hospital. I see the room where we will host friends in just a few days and the comfortable chair where I will settle in and read.

The experience of walking through the shuttered house, letting the light in, and embracing both memories and anticipations is a spatial version of the practice of sabbath reflection. We experience in our gentle practice the equivalent of attentively walking through the house. We remember worship from the week before and recall our days, starting with Sunday afternoon. We recall the parade of faces and the sequences of work that we named. We review what we know and imagine the week to come and ready ourselves to greet the week with our gentle practices.

In the introduction to *Aids to Reflection*, Coleridge defines what he means by Christian reflection. He asks us to imagine an eye that both registers and puts out light, and he claims that just such an eye is the eye of our soul. To exercise this eye of our soul is to reflect, and to reflect is a mode of thought that is divine. He quotes Saint Paul's claim that even in this earthly life, our soul is "a house not made with hands" (2 Corinthians 5:1) but instead by God, and then writes, in a style that includes italics and all capital letters,

> Nothing is wanted but the eye, which is the light
> of this house, the light which is the eye of the soul.
> This *seeing* light, this *enlightening* eye, is Reflection.
> It is more, indeed, than is ordinarily meant by that
> word; but it is what a *Christian* ought to mean by
> it, and to know too, whence it first came and still

continues to come—of what light even this light is *but* a reflection. This, too, is THOUGHT; and all thought is but unthinking that does not flow out of this, or tend towards it.[18]

The passage begins with the claim that the eye is the light of the house, which is the soul. We speak about someone who has a light in their eye, or a twinkle, and we mean it in the most benevolent and attractive way. A person with a genuine light in their eye is one with whom we would like to spend time. By contrast, we might feel pity or sorrow for those whose eyes are dull or dead, in whom the light has gone out. We look at them and might think that there is no *there* there. It can be exhausting to be around one where the brightness in the eye is a superficial flash—for example, the overly bright eye of one who has taken too much of a stimulating drug. We recognize that this light is not the real thing and bears the same relationship to the sun's light as the light from a neon strip. Light emerges from our eyes and is a gauge for the state of our soul.

Our images of the fontal light and reflection can give us full access to the richness that Coleridge invites us into. He writes that a Christian ought "to know too, whence it first came and still continues to come—of what light even this light is but a reflection." This is our image of the marble of water, lit by the sunset, the fontal light. And he writes of our eyes that they can be "this *seeing* light, this *enlightening* eye." This sort of seeing is made possible as we imagine our time of reflection like the compact mirror, putting a spotlight on our moments of grace and failure, those that have passed and those that are to come.

The final words of the prayer take seriously Jesus' invitation to abide in him and remind us that apart from him, we can do nothing.

In the name of Jesus, the light of the world.

As I seek to understand these words, I imagine a vineyard. Within walking distance of my diocese's retreat center, the Bishop's Ranch, is a vineyard. I have walked there and when no one is looking, eaten a grape. What remains on the vine is a little branch that held the fruit. The branch is connected to a vine that is connected to innumerable branches, which bear much fruit in the harvest season. Jesus, building on the imagery from Isaiah that God's people are like a vineyard that God has planted and nurtured, takes on the role of the branches, binding all people together.

These branches are utterly inseparable from the vine. One flows seamlessly into the other. Augustinian monk and author Martin Laird, a masterful teacher of the contemplative life, expands on Jesus' teaching that he is the vine and we are the branches. He asks us to imagine God is the ocean, and we are waves. And then to take the image even further, God is light, and we are a ray of that light.

Coleridge is again our companion and teacher. In the act of reflection, we can see glimpses of eternity and the infinite. He wrote to a friend,

> Reflexion seems the first approach to, and shadow
> of the divine Permanency; the first effort of the divine
> working in us to bind the Past and Future with the

Present, and thereby to let in upon us some faint glimmering of that State in which Past, Present and Future are co-adunated (united) in the adorable I AM.[19]

I teach and believe that Holy Eucharist is a foretaste of heaven. And I believe reflection is, by grace, a preview of heaven. Reflection in the light of Christ can be a "glimmering" of the divine permanency of eternal time, where we abide with "the Father of lights, with whom there is no variation or shadow due to change" (James 1:17). Whether we sit at home or in our church, we reflect on our past week, our present state, and our future week and catch some glimpse, from time to time and by grace, that these three are one.

Jesus is repeatedly identified with light in the Gospel of John. In the prologue, we are told that "the light shines in the darkness, and the darkness did not overcome it" (John 1:5). In the last teaching of his public ministry, he says, "I have come as light into the world, so that everyone who believes in me should not remain in the darkness" (John 12:46). In the middle of his public ministry, in the verse that inspired the conclusion of our prayer, he goes beyond metaphor and claims to be light. He says, "I am the light of the world, whoever follows me will never walk in darkness but will have the light of life" (John 8:12). In our earthly pilgrimage, darkness is all around us, but with Jesus, it cannot consume us.

Now that the prayer is firmly placed in your memory, it serves as the frame and focus for your prayer time. The prayer establishes your intention; use the rest of your time to follow through on your reflection. As with the practice of twenty minutes a day of prayer, it is important to find the best time and place for this gentle practice of praying and reflecting on the sabbath. I strongly recommend finding time before the Sunday worship service so that the practice is integrated into a whole experience of sabbath that includes Holy Eucharist. Taking time before worship begins helps us remember that we are one in Christ because we all share one bread and one cup.

In my life, the best time for this gentle practice is before the 8 a.m. service. I love arriving at church ten minutes earlier and taking time to simply sit in our sacred space, gaze at the altar, say the prayer, and then muse on the week that has just passed and the week that I expect. Others find the time and place that works best for them. For instance, Judy tried to pray and reflect on the sabbath before the 10 a.m. service, but the church is much busier then, and, as head of the altar guild, she was far too easy of a target for questions and concerns. She now says the prayer and spends time in reflection at home, before church. The important thing is to experiment until you find the time and place that works best for you.

The amount of time in reflection is likely to vary. At first, I set a timer for ten minutes and found that my mind stayed engaged with the work of reflection for nearly the whole time. I've since discovered, largely because I'm now in the habit of noticing the practices throughout the week, that I normally complete the full inventory in about five minutes or so. I no longer use a timer, but I am glad I set it when I first introduced this practice into my life.

This gentle practice of prayer and reflection is an essential step in receiving the gift of sabbath. In 2010, I took a sabbatical for several months. My friend and I designed parallel sabbaticals. We started with three weeks on pilgrimage on the Camino, returned to our respective homes where we did housework in a spirit of simplicity, and finally gathered our families together for a locally sourced meal. We applied for and received a grant to help financially support the sabbatical.

As part of the grant, we flew to Louisville, Kentucky, for a few days of formation in the Christian practice of sabbatical and sabbath. One of our teachers was Norman Wirzba, a professor of Old Testament. He asked us to reflect on the Hebrew word *menuha*, which means rest and delight. It is translated in the New Revised Standard Version as "rested" in Genesis, "so on the seventh day God finished the work that he had done, and he rested on the seventh day from all the work he had done" (Genesis 2:2). To help us embrace the full meaning of the word, he told us of his childhood in an agrarian community in the shadow of the Canadian Rockies. When he was growing up in the 1960s and 1970s, the whole community still observed the sabbath. Not only did that mean the practice of going to church, but it also meant rest from work. Their practice of observing the sabbath was the anchor for a life in balance, which included being profoundly in tune with the rhythms of nature. The farmers knew that the soil's natural fertility depends on a rhythm of both productivity and rest. The land, from time to time, must lie fallow.

Wirzba told us that the community has since changed. These days, few go to church, and none take a full sabbath. To make a living in modern agriculture requires that one work without ceasing. Further, the demands for output are so high that what the land produces through ordinary attention to natural rhythm and abundance is not enough. The land never lies fallow but is blanketed with ever more sophisticated chemicals that increase immediate output but diminish long-term fertility.

His story provides a keen insight into our lives today. Most of us work without ceasing, failing to rest and refresh. We might see immediate returns on our work, but eventually, the stress and strain take its toll on our health, relationships, and spiritual lives.

We are all aware of how out of balance our world seems. To allow our Sundays to be utterly consumed with activity is to refuse a gift of God. In Bible studies, people frequently puzzle over Jesus' relationship to the sabbath. He famously heals on the sabbath, angering the Pharisees, whose rules insist on no work at all. Yet Jesus does not reject the sabbath: he teaches that he fulfills the law, does not abolish it, and that the sabbath was made for humankind, not humankind for the sabbath (Mark 2:27). Jesus is clear: sabbath is a gift from God. To needlessly fill our sabbath with work and errands is to reject this gift. When we worship every Sunday and adopt the gentle practice of prayer and reflection on the sabbath, we make inroads on reclaiming the biblical gift of sabbath, and we take another step toward restoring peace and balance—in our lives and in the world.

THIS WEEK

On Sunday, before worship,
say the sabbath prayer and then reflect
on the last week and the week to come.

SHIFT

Reclaim the biblical teaching of the sabbath
and use it to integrate the
gentle practices into your life.

REPETITION

Once a week, at the same time and in the
same place, take ten minutes to reflect.

CAMINO BOOTS

Commit to weekly worship and
twenty minutes of prayer.

CHAPTER FIVE
Smile Your Secret Smile

GENTLE PRACTICE

Find your unique angelic smile and, when
no one is looking, smile your secret smile,
remembering that life is beautiful.

WORDS

Heart   Smile
Beauty   Gratitude
Acedia

*O God, send me this day to do the work
you have given me to do, to love and serve you
with gladness and singleness of heart.* Amen.

Smile Your Secret Smile

This week, we will focus on the word "heart" with a gentle practice of smiling your secret smile. This practice is an exercise of your mouth that can strangely, curiously warm your heart. You may remember the gospel story of the road to Emmaus when an unrecognized and resurrected Jesus appears alongside two of his followers while they are on the way from Jerusalem to Emmaus. This stranger talks to the two followers about many things, including stories about Jesus and their time together. And yet the two followers do not recognize him. They encourage the stranger to stay with them into the evening, and it is only when the stranger breaks the bread that they recognize Jesus. They then say, "Were not our hearts burning within us while he was talking to us on the road, while he was opening the scriptures to us?" (Luke 24:32). Other translations of the Bible say their hearts were strangely warmed. John Wesley, an eighteenth-century Anglican priest, was inspired to reform first his own life and then the life of the church after he had an experience where his "heart was strangely warmed," an echo of the disciples' experience on the road to Emmaus.

This week's practice is simply, from time to time, to smile a secret smile that you've learned how to make, inspired by saints, angels, and mystics. Now, let me caution you: it is not my experience that my heart is curiously warmed, and then I smile my secret smile. Rather, it is that, from time to time, no more than a few times a day, this gentle practice reminds me to stop and smile. I make sure that no one is around to see, and I smile my secret smile. My heart is warmed, and it is as though I am restored to myself. I see Beauty, give thanks, and then do the next work, whatever that happens to be.

I once introduced this practice to a group of people without mentioning that it is a secret. A young woman immediately cautioned me that I should be aware that women are told to smile more often than men in social situations because that is more likely to help them get what they want. Women are taught to use smiles as a way of gaining power automatically granted to men. All the more reason, for both men and women, to smile in secret. As with prayer, the primary relationship here is with God, who always already loves you. This is not a power play, but your secret smile is just one way to say thank you.

The secret smile has a literary inspiration and two visual inspirations. The literary inspiration is Dante's *Paradiso*. Dante is masterfully precise in his use of language, often mathematically so: if a word is repeated many times, Dante is making an important point. One of the words repeated most often in the *Paradiso* is a word that never occurs, without bitter irony, in the *Inferno* and rarely appears in the *Purgatorio*: this is the word "smile." In *Paradiso*, the smile is a sign of the peace, love, and friendship for the souls of the saints Dante meets in his pilgrimage across the cosmos. Many times, Dante writes that the smiles brighten as they welcome him, at least temporarily, into their fellowship. Their smiles reveal the gladness in the hearts of their souls.

You can arrange its muscles so that your mouth can give some hint of your future saintly smile when, with those who have gone before, you gaze on the face/faces of God. As Christians, we live in the tension of the already and the not yet. Already Christ is risen, and death is conquered; not yet do we live in the fullness of time when Christ becomes all in all. Christ has died. Christ is risen. Christ will come again. When we smile our secret smile, we lean into the Christ is risen part of the already and the not yet. As we search for our secret smile, we can think of the smiles of the saints in practice.

As you seek your secret smile, I offer two visual cues, one Christian and the other from ancient Greece. Almost all of the angels and saints' sculptures that adorn Gothic cathedrals have some variation of a solemn expression. Their expressions lend a certain dignity to those frequently sober spaces. The smiling angel in the Rheims Cathedral in France is a welcome variation. The statue depicts a human-inspired angel who offers a smile that suggests a divine and glorious secret. I first learned to smile an angelic smile by gazing at this image and smiling back.

The other visual source comes from ancient Greece. Early in the sixth century, in Athens and the other cities of Greece, the skill in creating the likeness of a human being took a stunning step forward. For decades, sculptures of a variety of men and women were created with a particular and mysterious smile known as the "archaic smile." There is no clear consensus on what the smile signifies. It may simply be that being happy was a sign of worldly success and those being sculpted wished to convey their worldly power. Some scholarship points to another possibility, linked to the Eleusinian Mysteries. Eleusis is thirteen miles to the east of Athens. Unlike Athens, where only freeborn males were citizens, in Eleusis, all who spoke Greek were free to become initiated into the Mysteries of Eleusis. Socrates was utterly devoted to the Mysteries, and, like every other significant figure of ancient Greece and Rome, he kept its secrets. While we don't have a full understanding of the Mysteries, we know that they involved Persephone and Demeter and had something to do with eternal life, perhaps connected to the renewal of life in the season of spring. The Roman writer Seneca observed, "The Mysteries are not something that can be owned, like a thought; they are not something that can be applied, like a formula. They are a place that offers some further thing each time people return."[20] Perhaps people often walked the thirteen miles back to Athens with an enigmatic smile on their faces, inspiring the sculptures on which we still gaze.

As we explore our smile, I'd like for us to hold two words: beauty and gratitude. When I first taught the gentle practices to a group of clergy, this teaching was a point of concern. In a later conversation, the bishop worried that an emphasis on beauty would only reinforce our reliance on what I call the American Cult of Lifestyle. The word "beautiful" connotes a luxurious handbag or car; he worried that the word had been corrupted by secular use and wouldn't translate well in a Christian context. The bishop has an excellent point, so I want to flag the problem upfront and be very clear that what I am asking you to consider is real Beauty with a capital "B." As a working theory, imagine that there is such a thing as perfect Beauty, and that all that is truly beautiful participates in that perfect Beauty. Imagine that Beauty is not simply a name we give to a concept but is a deep truth of God's reality.

To anchor our sense of Beauty, think of the most beautiful worship services you have ever participated in, times when you, along with all the others in the room, worshiped God with sights, sounds, smells, and movements. The Beauty in such services is likely to be in both the smiles and the tears, in the joy and the sorrow. I experienced such Beauty on the first Sunday that shelter in place began in response to the COVID-19. I led worship in our sacred space with a small crew. I prayed the whole Eucharistic Prayer A from *The Book of Common Prayer*, held up the chalice and paten, and said, "The gifts of God for the people of God," into a camera, but then I was the only one to eat the bread and drink the wine. A quartet from our choir, singing at a social distance, then sang a Renaissance motet. I sat in a chair to the side of the altar and wept. It was both a moment of Beauty and achingly sad. In a season where we all want to tap into our deepest sources of comfort, we are forbidden from participating in that which God gave to comfort and strengthen us most.

This moment of liturgical Beauty was also a moment of divine Truth and Goodness. We were still remembering what Jesus asked us to remember, that he died for us and gave himself for us because he loves us. We did this in remembrance of him, recognizing that the love that suffused our ritual is still True even when we couldn't do it in its fullness. In *The Book of Common Prayer*, the rubric or instructions in the ministration to the sick specifies that those who are unable to receive because of "extreme sickness" are to be assured "that all benefits of Communion are received, even though the Sacrament is not received with the mouth." The communion is still real and True. Further, to not share with hands and mouth in a pandemic season is also to participate in the Good. I love my brothers and sisters in Christ and wish them to thrive. I will not put them at needless risk of infection.

This is one example of the reality that what is truly Beautiful is also Good and True. Beauty, Truth, and Goodness are the three classic areas of study in philosophy. As Christians, we believe these three essential attributes are revealed in God through our scriptures and sacraments. To discover your secret angelic smile, imagine that these three are one, like the three persons of the Trinity are one. While the three are always distinct, they also so thoroughly interconnect with each other that they are one. We are already familiar with this at some level. A physicist describes a solution to a difficult problem created by a colleague as elegant or beautiful. A beautiful sculpture is said to capture the true likeness of a human being. A passionate reformer turns our attention to an ugly truth we would rather not see and inspires us to take action such that goodness triumphs over evil, and when former adversaries embrace, we cry because the reconciliation is Beautiful.

I believe these links among Beauty, Truth, and Goodness are always available to us, but our twenty-first-century American minds are, by cultural habit, weak at seeing and celebrating the connections. The muscles of our perceiving minds have atrophied, and it is up to each of us individually to recover the capacity to realize once again the Truth. The work this week is to begin deliberately looking for Beauty in this holy and higher sense and to respond or remember with a smile. We may resist here because believing in Beauty, Truth, and Goodness is no less a leap of faith than believing that Jesus was resurrected.

Our teacher Coleridge offers this response to those skeptical of Christianity, which applies just as well to the reality of Beauty, Truth, and Goodness.

> I should expect to hear a troubled Murmur: How can
> I comprehend this? How is this to be proved? To the
> first question, I should answer: Christianity is not a
> Theory, or a Speculation; but a *Life*. Not a *Philosophy*
> of Life, but a Life and a living Process. To the second:
> TRY IT.[21]

Coleridge's advice rings true today: try living as though these exalted forms of Beauty are invitations to live in the Truth as Good people. Our capacity to smile our secret smile is one way that we say yes to this invitation from God.

As a practical matter, I encourage us to trust our intuition. We know when our lives are noisy, distracted, impatient, angry, and ugly. And we know when our lives are focused, serene, harmonious, generous, and Beautiful. We know when we have been fully alive and when we have been alienated. We gradually learn to trust that deep sense in ourselves. This gentle practice offers a new way in our sabbath reflection to remember the past week and anticipate the week to come. This practice invites us to ask: Has our last week been Beautiful? It may be the case that a week filled with suffering and grief is seen in retrospect to be suffused with Beauty because of the tenderness, vulnerability, and intimacy that the suffering produced. It may be that a week filled with worldly triumph seems ugly in the light of reflection. What felt like confidence at the moment now appears as vain puffing-up.

One way to test true Beauty and whether or not we are responding to it well is the depth of our gratitude. The appropriate response to Beauty is gratitude. It is fitting to give thanks when one encounters Beauty. As we slowly enter into this mystery of the secret smile, we are invited to embrace a Christian truth that all of life is a gift. As King David says to God, "For all things come from you, and of your own have we given you" (1 Chronicles 29:14). Furthermore, as we both receive and give, remember, "Every generous act of giving, with every perfect gift, is from above, coming down from the Father of lights, with whom there is no variation or shadow due to change" (James 1:17). Theologian and country parson George Herbert was particularly attuned to this truth of God's blessings in his daily life. Whenever given a compliment on something he did, whether it was for a sermon, an act of pastoral kindness, or one of his immortal poems, he responded, "less than the least of God's mercies."[22]

An ongoing sense of gratitude is a sign that we are beginning to live with gladness and singleness of heart. A mere attitude of gratitude is not enough. We are invited, over time, to *be* gratitude. Another name for ongoing gratitude is adoration, which is exactly the word we use to describe the eternal life of the angels and saints in heaven. Our secret smile is our own foretaste of the adoration our souls will give, God willing, for eternity.

Tanner, one of the small-group members, was drawn deeply to this practice and found a highly practical use for it. Some time ago, he was part of a small group that read ancient spiritual advice. Among these was the *Praktikos* of Evagrius Ponticus.

Evagrius was a worldly man of fourth-century Constantinople who, after a scandal, fled to Jerusalem and then to the desert. He learned from the Desert Fathers and Mothers and then produced books of sayings that captured their wisdom along with his perspective. Evagrius is particularly clear that our thoughts matter, and he offers astute insight about the mind games that plague us. Among the gifts of Evagrius is the first draft of what was eventually called the Seven Deadly Sins. Six of the seven sins articulated by Evagrius can be described in familiar words, captured by Dante and understood by us today: pride, envy, wrath, avarice, gluttony, and lust. But Dante calls the seventh deadly sin "sloth," a word that fails to capture what Evagrius means by the sin of *acedia*. Ordinarily, Evagrius writes concise sentences and paragraphs in his collections of spiritual advice. In the case of *acedia*, he writes a short story, apparently believing there is no better way than narrative to capture the reality of the deadly sin of *acedia*. Evagrius writes,

> The demon of *acedia*—also called the noonday demon (Ps. 91:5)—is the one that causes the most serious trouble of all. He presses his attack upon the monk in the early afternoon and besieges the soul until the early evening. First of all, he makes it seem that the sun barely moves, if at all, and that the day is fifty hours long. Then he constrains the monk to look constantly out the windows, to walk outside the cell, to gaze carefully at the sun to determine how far it stands from dinnertime, to look now this way and now that to see if perhaps one of the brothers appears from his cell. Then too, he instills in the heart of the monk a hatred for the place, a hatred for his very life itself, a hatred for manual labor. He leads him to reflect that charity

has departed from among the brothers, that there is no one to give encouragement. Should there be someone at this period who happens to offend him in some way or other, this too the demon uses to contribute further to his hatred. This demon drives him along to desire other sites where he can more easily procure life's necessities, more readily find work and make a real success of himself. He goes on to suggest that, after all, it is not the place that is the basis of pleasing the Lord. God is to be adored everywhere. He joins to these reflections the memories of his dear ones and of his former way of life. He depicts life stretching out for a long period of time, and brings before the mind's eye the toil of the ascetic struggle and, as the saying has it, leaves no leaf unturned to induce the monk to forsake his cell and drop out of the fight.[23]

One of our small-group members, Tanner works in insurance in the city and found he could easily swap out his cubicle for the monk's cell, his co-workers for the brothers, and the various temptations of his computer as an outward manifestation of the inward restlessness of his mind. I join Tanner, and I suspect you do too, in having some period of time every afternoon when my thoughts resemble the thoughts of this monk besieged by the demon of *acedia*.

This teaching of Evagrius concludes, "No other demon follows close upon the heel of this one when he is defeated, but only a state of deep peace and inexpressible joy arise out of this struggle."[24] Tanner discovered that, from time to time, when he found himself caught up in the thoughts and feelings of *acedia*, smiling his secret smile brought him back to his center and reminded him of who he is, made in the image and likeness of God. Remembering that we are body and soul, Tanner found that the gesture of the body—the mouth's slight turn up and into an enigmatic smile—was enough to warm the heart and chase away, at least for a moment, the demon of *acedia*.

Tanner's use of the smile to battle afternoon doldrums invites two caveats. First, if we used the smile every time we had a bored thought, our life would be like whack-a-mole with constant smiles that would soon wear out their effectiveness. The smile keeps its potency only if used with discretion and attention. The second caveat is that Evagrius actually overstates the effect of triumphing over the demon of *acedia*. Even for Evagrius, it is not the case that "no other demon follows close upon the heel of this one." In fact, triumph over the demon and the "deep peace and inexpressible joy" invite a final sneaky demon, a variation of pride Evagrius calls "vainglory." Vainglory in this case might be the thought, "I just triumphed over my *acedia*! I must be so spiritually mature!" Whenever we smile our secret smile, feel our hearts curiously warmed, and remember Beauty and adoration, it can be tempting to think we are pretty great. But remember, it is all gift, and whatever just occurred to us is "less than the least of God's mercies."

Find your unique angelic smile and, when no one is looking, smile your secret smile, remembering that life is beautiful.

THIS WEEK

Find your unique angelic smile and, when no one is looking, smile your secret smile, remembering that life is beautiful.

SHIFT

Have faith that Beauty, Truth, and Goodness are real—and that our world participates in all three.

REPETITION

Regularly, throughout each day, notice Beauty and always give thanks to God.

CAMINO BOOTS

Commit to weekly worship and twenty minutes of prayer.

SABBATH PRAYER

O God, in your light we see light; help me reflect on the week that has passed, that I may remember in truth, and on the week to come, that I may be ready to do all such good works as thou hast prepared for me to walk in, in the name of Jesus, the light of the world. Amen.

CHAPTER SIX
Use Your Wound

GENTLE PRACTICE

Imagine that you have an open wound in your side, like the resurrected Jesus, and that, just as God sent Jesus wounded, we are sent wounded. We are to use our wounds.

WORDS

Send Me   Open Wound

Sorrow

*O God, send me this day to do the work
you have given me to do, to love and serve you
with gladness and singleness of heart.* Amen.

Use Your Wound

Our daily prayer begins, "O God, *send me* this day to do the work you have given me to do…" In previous weeks, we focused on the words gladness, singleness, and heart from this prayer; this week, we will again draw from the prayer but with a focus on the words: Send me. This phrase draws upon Jesus' teaching in the Gospel of John, "as the Father has sent me, so I send you" (John 20:21). The context of Jesus' teaching here is important. After Jesus' death on the cross, the disciples are gathered in a locked room for fear of the authorities. The resurrected Jesus appears, with his wounds visible, and says "peace" twice. Then after he tells them, "as the Father has sent me, so I send you," Jesus breathes on them, bestowing the Holy Spirit.

The gentle practice of this week is to imagine that Jesus sends us to do our work in peace, accompanied by the Holy Spirit, and with our wounds. Just as God sent Jesus back into the world with his wounds, so we are sent into each day with our wounds. The practice of being sent into the world with an open wound has deep resonance with the core of the Christian story, and we will explore much of that resonance in this chapter, but first, I share a story of how I used the wound in my side.

I believe it is largely true that most of what we need to know to be a good person we learn in kindergarten. When my sons were in kindergarten, their teachers taught them to use a compliment sandwich, a great technique at any age. This means that you surround a criticism of a person's behavior with thoughtful observations about what a person does well. "I'm so glad we share lunch on a regular basis. Please ask me before you eat one of my potato chips. It's fun to be your friend." There you have it: a compliment sandwich. I try and practice this technique as a husband, father, and rector, and I often mention this approach in sermons to encourage the St. Paul's community to be both honest and kind. A couple of weeks into the shelter-in-place directives of the COVID-19 pandemic, I received an email that was a perfect compliment sandwich. The email began with what a good man I am and how I had done a great job leading our church community through the transition, particularly with worship on Facebook Live. It ended with a kind and generous review of some of the ways I had moved and inspired this person in the past. And then, in the middle, there was the meat of the matter.

This parishioner and the parishioner's partner wanted me to preach from the heart more—to more directly name the feelings we were all experiencing during this time of profound disorientation. They were looking for emotional consolation that I was not providing for them. The meat of this sandwich cut me to the quick, rendering me almost unable to read the bread part of the compliment sandwich. My mind spun out all sorts of reasons that the two sermons I had given so far were in the right vein. But I knew myself well enough not to write this person back until my initial defensive reactions settled down. So using this week's gentle practice, I placed the pain and confusion in the wound in my side, trusting that what the parishioner wrote was not in the spirit of a soldier stabbing the side of a dying man but the curious and wondering exploration from a friend.

Two days later, I was finally able to write a response. Before I sent it, I asked my wife to read it. She had previously read the parishioner's email and found it thoughtful and kind, which I could theoretically see was true, but the wounding observations weren't about her! She read my first response and commented that it read like it was written with clenched teeth. "That's because it was!" I said. My response had gone down from my head, skipped over my heart, and settled in my angry gut. I set aside the email for one more day, while I continued to pray and attend to the open and vulnerable wound in my side. The next day, in my morning prayers, I was given the gift of a sense of humor and a way to playfully connect the parishioner's observation to the teachings of Jesus. I promptly wrote and sent the email, which concluded with a genuine expression of thanksgiving. I know this person wants me to thrive and wants the best for the congregation of St. Paul's. I knew that in my head right away. It took me three days, lots of prayer, and this gentle practice of using the wound in my side to know it in my heart and gut. In their typical, thoughtful way, the parishioner and the parishioner's spouse sent supportive emails in the weeks that followed as I made exactly the adjustment in my preaching they had been hoping for.

The gentle practice of using our wound builds on our daily prayer as well as our commitment to being in community with one another, accountable and responsible to the words of Jesus, who says, "as the Father sent me, so I send you." Our work in the Christian community is to get to know each other and to build trust so that we can begin to do for one another as my wife did for me when I was faced with the benevolent yet painful email. It hurts to be hurt, and the pain can often blind us to the times and places where the hurt is an invitation, even from God, to grow in love. This gentle practice of using our wound requires the loving guidance and support of others. We pray, look at a face as a PERSON, and smile our angelic smile in secret. But if we always use our wound in secret, we will very likely go astray. We must take good care of our open wound. And we have both medical—and theological—evidence that leaving a wound open can be a healthy practice.

As a child, I often got scrapes and cuts. Eventually, I figured out that, after cleaning the wound, it was often best to leave it open to the air. Tightly bandaged wounds stayed moist and so often stayed raw longer. If I could either dress the wound very lightly or, even better, leave it exposed without further damage, the wound healed more quickly, developing a scab that later peeled off to reveal tender skin. Theologian and poet Søren Kierkegaard wrote: "Keeping open a wound can indeed also be healthy—a healthy and open wound—at times it is worse when it closes."[25] I shared this quote with my friend Teresa for whom it was literally true. She had some cancerous cells taken out of the skin at her hairline. The surgeon opted to leave the wound open. When Teresa asked why he didn't stitch it closed, he explained that, if he did, she would have a perpetual look of curiosity, with one eyebrow raised. The wound eventually healed naturally, with her forehead retaining its full expressive potential. In the case of our gentle practice, we are to imagine that the wound is always open and always will be, just like the wound in the side of the resurrected Jesus.

This gentle practice of using my wound is intensely kinesthetic, imaginative, and emotional. As I have embraced this practice and lived with my wound, it is revealing a sorrow in me that is far larger than me, as though my body is too small to contain it. This expansive sorrow is revealed to my emotional intuition most clearly when I go on long walks and the concerns of the day gradually recede. I have learned, when I return to this sorrow, to just dwell with it, with a swelling of near tears that has yet to spill over. It is a sorrow without words, beyond what my mind can comprehend and my heart can fully embrace.

I wonder if I am slowly being ushered into an ancient spiritual truth. The Greek-speaking mothers and fathers of the desert and the urban theologians who loved and supported them spoke and wrote of a faculty of spiritual knowing they called the *nous*. In English translations, *nous* is often rendered as "intellect," which is misleading because we think of intellectuals as people with head knowledge but not necessarily knowledge of the heart. By contrast, *nous*, as used by these spiritual masters, means a faculty that fuses the head and the heart and goes beyond them, into the incomprehensible depths of the God of our salvation.

Because of the potential depth and breadth of this practice, it might be helpful to skirt the edges of this gentle practice until you feel invited into it. It may take some years of a prayer practice and a long season of being in a discipleship group or working with a trusted spiritual director until you are drawn into this work of using your wound. Although sorrow, sadness, and hurt can be a necessary invitation to intimacy, vulnerability, and love, they can also be a path to bitterness and needless pain. We all need a robust prayer life and friends to help us distinguish between the two.

As we seek to understand this gentle practice in our lives, allow me to offer three perspectives on wounds and Jesus: We wound Jesus; Jesus is always coming to us wounded; and Jesus sends us wounded and to be wounded.

We Wound Jesus

Holy Week is the most important week of the church year. By walking together through the events of Jesus' passion we learn more than words alone could ever teach us about the meaning of Jesus' life and death. For this one week, at least, we are no longer merely gazing with admiration at a great teacher and inspiring leader; we are following his footsteps as though we were the crowd, a follower, religious authority, or a soldier. On Palm Sunday, we begin the journey like the adoring but fickle crowd that welcomed Jesus into Jerusalem. We rejoice and wave, but just an hour later, we sing a song that I have yet to be able to sing all the way through because, at some point, I always just choke up. Very often, I choke up at these words:

> Who was the guilty? Who brought this upon thee?
> Alas my treason, Jesus hath undone thee.
> 'Twas I, Lord Jesus, I it was denied thee.
> I crucified thee.

At my congregation, beginning with Ash Wednesday, we have a dish filled with large horse nails. People are invited to take one of the nails and keep it throughout Lent, using it as a way to reflect on their sin. On Good Friday, I bring in a very heavy and large wooden cross and lay it on the floor, just in front of the rood screen and altar. In silence, people are invited to come up and hammer their nail into the cross. Nearly everyone in the church participates. As we pound the nail into the wood, sometimes with great force, we acknowledge that we, like the soldiers, have wounded Jesus. *I crucified thee.*

Throughout the events of Holy Week, Jesus is surrounded by people who hurt him—and those people are us. Judas betrays him, Peter denies him, and the rest of the disciples, who choose to sleep through his night of anguish, abandon him. The authorities, both secular and religious, manipulate things in order to condemn him while the previously adoring crowds call for blood. With gestures that could be taken from today's videos of over-militarized cops, the soldiers beat him, spit on him, and flay him. And yes, they nail him to the tree. We do all these things ourselves. We are the disciples. We are the jeering crowd and the cruel soldiers far more often than we are the women faithfully watching at a distance. We know that, somehow, somewhere, we are implicated in the story we recreate each year.

The wound Jesus shows to his followers is a wound his followers helped make. The power of the whole story of the passion is that it casts a broad net of human behavior. I remember a friend of mine and I were driving to a concert once in college where we were going to sing. After a period of companionable silence, he turned to me and asked, "Do you ever have the experience of remembering something you did and then wincing at the memory?" I replied, "Yes," and felt immeasurably relieved that someone else had an experience I lived then on a regular basis. We all have memories that make us cringe. Even deep into the Christian pilgrimage, those memories don't go entirely away. We have not always treated people with compassion and kindness. When we are mean and contemptuous, even in the small acts of snarky laughs and righteous bombast, it is not just the direct victims of our dismissive anger that feel the wound. Jesus also feels this wound, but he does not retaliate. Rather through great love and mercy, he forgives. This gentle practice of using our wound is humble because it starts with the truthful recognition that not only do we hurt but also we cause hurt. Not only does Jesus know this about us but also he takes the hurt we cause into himself.

Jesus Comes to Us Wounded

A classic Bible study is to read the Gospel of Mark over several weeks, starting at the beginning and ending in the eighth chapter, at exactly the midway point. By that time, the study has covered a variety of stories and teachings of Jesus. In the eighth chapter, the study takes on a profound question as Jesus asks his followers, "Who do you say that I am?"

If we are serious about growing in faith throughout our lives, we ought never to stop asking this question. In Mark, Peter boldly answers, "You are the Messiah" (Mark 8:29). Jesus cautions his followers to tell no one, which is a sign that Peter appears to have the right answer.

Martha's answer to the same kind of question in the Gospel of John teaches another equally profound lesson for all who wish to follow Jesus. Martha often gets a bad reputation as being more superficial than her sister Mary. In Luke 10:38-42, she bustles around with the work of hospitality while Mary enjoys the better part of sitting at Jesus' feet and beholding him. In every church I have served, many women have told me, at one point or another, they are Martha, not Mary, and their words always land on my ear as a self-deprecating comment. In the Gospel of John, Martha is redeemed. Keeping in character, she is the one to go out and meet Jesus when he is on his way to Bethany to bring her brother Lazarus back from the dead. As he approaches the tomb, they have a conversation where Jesus reveals that he is resurrection. He concludes by asking Martha, "Do you believe this?" She responds in a way that slipped by my attention for years but finally rocked me back on my proverbial heels. She says, "Yes, Lord, I believe that you are the Messiah, the Son of God, the one coming into the world" (John 11:27). The first two titles, Messiah and Son of God, affirm her faith in much the same way that Peter's response in Mark affirms his. The third title—"the one coming into the world"—invites me to slow down and admire Martha's insight. It's a peculiar thing to say. Jesus is standing right in front of her. What does she mean that he is the one coming into the world? Apparently, he is already there.

I believe Jesus is always the one coming into the world. In Hebrews, we hear, "Jesus Christ is the same yesterday and today and forever" (Hebrews 13:8). By using the gerund "coming," Martha captures one of the most essential mysteries about Jesus, one that we articulate together in the responsive words in Eucharistic Prayer A, "Christ has died. Christ is risen. Christ will come again" (*The Book of Common Prayer*, p. 363). Jesus is both the risen one now and the one who is coming again, and both of these things are always true. Paul toggles back and forth between boldly proclaiming what God has *already* done in Jesus and what is *not yet* fulfilled. In these in-between times, we are to stay alert. Jesus is now, in the moment you read these words, the coming one, just as he was to Martha two thousand years ago. He is still coming. Once we embrace this mysteriously indeterminate reality of the already and the not yet, we have a lens on the New Testament that gives us great interpretive power. Many of the passages in Paul that seem impossibly convoluted take on clarity as we realize that Paul is negotiating between the freedom of the already and the not yet of our sinful selves. In his letter to the Corinthians, Paul masterfully walks the theological tight rope between the freedom of the already and the obligation of the not yet. A clear example is at the conclusion of his great hymn to love in 1 Corinthians, where he writes, "For now we see in a mirror, dimly, but then we will see face to face" (1 Corinthians 13:12). We can, already, in this life, if only dimly, make out the Truth, Beauty, and Goodness of God. At the same time, we know that we have not yet known the fullness of God's Truth, Beauty and Goodness. The fullness is still coming.

As the coming one, Jesus always appears with his wounds. The Messiah's wounds are an essential part of his story. Isaiah t'was foretold it. In the longest of what we now call Isaiah's servant songs, passages that predict in great detail Jesus' passion, we are told that by his wounds, we are healed (Isaiah 53:5). The wounds Jesus receives go beyond the classic five wounds: the two in his hands, the two in his feet, and the one in his side. They include the gouges in his head from the crown of thorns, the slashes in his back from the thirty-nine lashes of the whip, and, if we follow the classic stations of the cross, the cuts and bruises from his three falls as he carries his cross from the site of his trial to Golgotha. And this list doesn't even include the emotional wounds of betrayal, abandonment, denial, scorn, and contempt. We are taught that even at the end of time, Jesus will appear to us wounded, eternally wounded. In his Revelation, John the Divine sees "between the throne and the four living creatures and among the elders a Lamb standing as if it had been slaughtered" (Revelation 5:6). Martha sees Jesus is the coming one. Isaiah sees the Messiah is the wounded one, and John the Divine sees the Messiah is eternally wounded. As followers of Jesus, we are always both healed and wounded. The gentle practice of using our wounds is a way to keep our attention on the profound truth that our Lord is wounded, and so are we. Suffering is not sin.

Of all the wounds on Jesus' body, the wound on his side is the focus of our gentle practice. It might help to have an image in mind as we talk about this wound. I recommend searching online and in a library for the sculpture "Christ and Saint Thomas" by the Renaissance artist Andrea del Verrochio. In this masterpiece, the wound on Jesus' side is clear. Jesus' arm is raised, revealing the wound to his disciple, Thomas. The raised arm shows a vulnerability but is also a gesture of authority and proclamation. Jesus appears both wounded and powerful to save.

The wound on Jesus' side is also the one in which we most regularly engage. The Gospel of John recounts how water and blood pour out of Jesus' wound. The soldier who stabs him in the side is following crucifixion protocol, using the measure to determine whether Jesus is dead or merely unconscious. The cross kills by asphyxiation or by a prolonged rapid heartbeat that causes hypovolemic shock. Either cause of death creates a buildup of fluid around the human heart. The water and the blood pouring from Jesus' side give visual affirmation that he is dead.

In the practice of the Episcopal Church, we see water and wine poured into a chalice and blessed such that it becomes to us Jesus' blood. We then drink from that chalice and hear the words, "the blood of Christ, the cup of salvation." The Johannine literature is clear that we participate in the life of Jesus through both the blood and the water. Deepening even further our connection with Jesus' wound in the side, the author of the first letter of John writes, "This is the one who came by water and blood, Jesus Christ, not with water only but with the water and the blood. And the Spirit is the one that testifies, for the Spirit is the truth. There are three that testify: the Spirit and the water and the blood, and these three agree" (1 John 5:6-8). It is Jesus' wound that makes possible our sharing of the water and the blood—and the testimony of the Spirit.

Jesus Sends Us Wounded and To Be Wounded

Jesus sends his followers with their wounds to use their wounds to heal, just as he used his wounds to heal. In some famous cases, the wounds are visible and known. Saint Francis of Assisi famously prayed to share in Jesus' suffering and so received the stigmata, wounds in his hands, feet, and side in imitation of Jesus. A famous twentieth-century Franciscan monk, Padre Pio, prayed for and received the same wounds. He was a simple man whose advice was to "pray, hope, and don't worry." He has been made a saint by the Roman Catholic Church and is unofficially the patron saint of stress relief and winter blues. Some sources say more Italians pray to Padre Pio than to any other figure because they have found he decreases their anxiety. By his wounds, others find themselves healed.

From the start, those with Jesus are wounded. In the Gospel of Luke, Simeon says to Mary, who is with the little child Jesus, "This child is destined for the falling and rising of many in Israel, and to be a sign that will be opposed so that the inner thoughts of many will be revealed—and a sword will pierce your own soul too" (Luke 2:34-35). Many of the most famous images of Mary try to capture precisely this wound in her soul. These include images of the Pietà, where Mary holds Jesus' dead body, and the crucifixion, where she is by his side. Even in depictions of her with the baby Jesus, artists capture her foreknowledge that he will suffer and die. From the beginning of her life as Jesus' mother, Mary is a wounded soul.

Paul, the model of a mature Christian, accepts that his earthly life following Jesus inevitably includes his wounds. He prays to have a thorn in his flesh removed and is told by God, "My grace is sufficient for you, for power is made perfect in weakness" (2 Corinthians 12:9). Suffering is a part of his internal struggle and his external mission. In his letter to the Colossians, Paul writes, "I am now rejoicing in my sufferings for your sake, and in my flesh I am completing what is lacking in Christ's afflictions for the sake of his body, that is, the church" (Colossians 1:24). By his wounds, Paul continues the earthly ministry of Jesus.

When we use our wounds, we follow in the footsteps of Francis, Pio, Mary, Paul, and countless other followers of Christ. We imagine a wound in our side like the wound of Jesus, a wound that passes through our skin and between our ribs to pierce our hearts. When I was a child, the tip of the middle finger of my right hand was severed while playing with a dangerous object on a beach. I was taken to the emergency room, where the tip was reattached, and gradually, of its own vitality, it reconnected itself. To this day, the tip of that finger is smaller than its opposite on my left hand; it lacks a nail, and, when the temperature is low, it is the first place on my body to go numb. It is a wound I carry with me at all times. Sometimes I am conscious of it, but often I am not. Just as awareness of the tip of my wounded finger comes and goes but never quite leaves me, so it is with my wounded heart. Following Jesus, it is how I am in the world. My body has a permanent wound in its right hand, and my soul has a permanent wound in its side.

This wound in the side can be protected and comforted. Crossing our arms over our chest is a gesture of great comfort. It makes us feel protected and safe. When we imagine the wound in our side, we find that our arms and hands now cover the wound. Further, with our hands and arms across our chest, we can haven ourselves. Havening is a primal gesture of stroking our upper arms from the shoulders down to the elbows. Like the practice of drawing a deep breath and allowing the exhale to take longer than the inhale, the physical practice of havening ourselves decreases the physical symptoms of anxiety and stress. As we slowly grow attentive to this imaginary wound in our side, we can both protect and comfort this wound.

Using our wound is a way to grow in love. This is because the wound abides in us whether life is difficult and sad or centered and joyful, and so we are ready to love others in whatever state they happen to be. My friends Karen and Brian, even when young, embraced this profound Christian truth. Together they were a pillar of the 20s/30s group I led at a church in Los Angeles. Our group met every Tuesday night for activities and conversation, and we always concluded the evening with the Compline service from *The Book of Common Prayer*. When Karen and Brian became engaged, an older couple in the parish generously commissioned the assistant organist to compose a new piece for their wedding. They chose the beautiful words of the collect from Compline inspired by the prayers of Saint Augustine.

> *Keep watch, dear Lord, with those who work or watch or weep this night, and give your angels charge over those who sleep. Tend the sick, Lord Christ; give rest to the weary, bless the dying, soothe the suffering, pity the afflicted, shield the joyous; and all for your love's sake.* Amen.[26]

They explained that they wanted to remind themselves and everyone gathered for their wedding that even at that joyous moment, there were people suffering in the world. Their marriage was easily one of the most joyful events in which I have ever participated. The church was packed, not only with family and friends but also with parishioners. As the warm music of the original composition washed over us, our hearts expanded in love, and our joy deepened.

We cannot expect that, in this life, there will ever be a time when we are not carrying wounds. Our wounds will be with us from now until the hour of our death. But we can grow in hope and confidence that, by grace and in love, God is using our wounds like Jesus used his own wounds. Through our wounds, as we seek to imitate the life of Jesus, we pray some may be healed. As we integrate our wounds into our daily work, we can be confident that we are participating in the life of Jesus. Theologian Catherine Pickstock writes that in this work, "We can prove the reality of atoning work in the integrity of a...style which endures and foils evil, anxiety, and tragedy with a saving fortitude and a joyful ultimate confidence."[27]

THIS WEEK

Imagine that you have an open wound in your side, like the resurrected Jesus, and that, just as God sent Jesus wounded, we are sent wounded. We are to use our wounds.

SHIFT

Do not be afraid to feel pain and sorrow, trusting that God will use your wounded heart to bring healing and love.

REPETITION

Find times of quiet to identify the ache in your heart and feel, without words or judgment, the simple feeling of sorrow.

SABBATH PRAYER

O God, in your light we see light; help me reflect on the week that has passed, that I may remember in truth, and on the week to come, that I may be ready to do all such good works as thou hast prepared for me to walk in, in the name of Jesus, the light of the world. Amen.

CHAPTER SEVEN
Name Your Home

GENTLE PRACTICE

Identify yourself as a pilgrim and give a name
to your home, your ultimate destination.

WORDS

Pilgrim   Home
Thin Spaces   Journeys
Songs   Word

O God, send me this day to do the work
you have given me to do, to love and serve you
with gladness and singleness of heart. Amen.

Name Your Home

When Judy learned the gentle practice of look at each face, she was reminded of one of the most beautiful things she ever experienced. One winter day, she was visiting her sister, who lives just north of Seattle. On an overcast day, they went together to a local farmer's market. As is very often the case in the Pacific Northwest, they were in the midst of a stretch of several weeks where the sky was perpetually leaden grey with light rain and no hint of the sun. As Judy was shopping for fruits and vegetables, the sun broke through the clouds, and at that moment, everyone—shoppers and vendors alike—stopped what they were doing and, in silence, turned their faces to the sun. At that moment, people were as unified as a field of sunflowers in turning toward the light.

The goal of this last chapter is to help you, body and soul, to be as fully drawn to the light of God as those at the farmers market were drawn to the light of the sun. This gentle practice of naming your home and being drawn toward the light of God is an exercise in hope. The ancient spiritual master Saint Diadochos defined hope as "the flight of the intellect in love toward that for which it hopes."[28] I invite you to use the imaginative part of your intellect to name and envision the place where you hope your soul will be after your death. You will know you have conceived of the right place when you find that your heart longs to be there. Dare to imagine a spiritual place where you would love to be and then long for it with your heart and mind. And, as you long for it with your heart and mind, claim for yourself that you are exercising the biblical virtue of hope.

We begin with identifying ourselves as pilgrims, as people on our way toward a spiritual home, with our spiritual face, the face of our soul always turned toward the true source of light. Some of us may have grown up in the church, having learned at least the basics of Jesus, while others may have grown up at some distance from the church and all its practices. Either way, when we leave our childhood home, we can choose the level of our participation in the spiritual life. Many of us live for years with minimal involvement in the way of Jesus until something or someone invites us to engage in spiritual practices — and we accept the invitation. As we commit to daily prayer and weekly worship, we begin our journey from being a seeker of God to a disciple. A disciple is one who is at least somewhat disciplined in practicing the practices.

In the course of reading this book, as you have said the daily prayer and practiced the gentle practices, you have been a disciple of Jesus. Now we shift from being a disciple to being a pilgrim. But where are you going?

Throughout your time with this book, you have gradually taken on a series of gentle practices. You have claimed that the work is very near you. You have committed to looking at each face and naming each work. You are praying and reflecting on the sabbath and smiling your secret smile. You are using your wound. Now, you are ready to name the goal of your earthly pilgrimage and to live your life as though each moment is another step in the direction of your spiritual home. Most teachers of Christian meditation encourage practitioners to find a prayer word or phrase. You then use that word or phrase to ever so gently nudge aside the thoughts that inevitably emerge during times of prayer and meditation. A simple, one-syllable word is often recommended, such as love, God, or Lord. Some might prefer the name of Jesus or the full Jesus prayer, "Lord Jesus Christ, Son of the Living God, have mercy on me, a sinner." The point is to pick a word or phrase and stick with it. Although each of these recommended words has great spiritual depth and meaning, they aren't intended as the focus of the reflection. Rather, let the word be and simply dwell with it. The same advice holds true for naming the goal of your earthly pilgrimage. Name your home and stick with it.

As the writer of Hebrews demonstrates in the climactic passage of his letter, the names and features of the spiritual home of a Christian pilgrim can assume many and diverse features. It can be a mountain like Athos, Sinai, or Zion. It can be a city like Canterbury, Campostela, or Jerusalem. It can be a heavenly event or location like a feast or a choir or Dante's celestial rose. For this final practice, the point is to pick a word or phrase for your soul's destination and make it your own. Giving your destination a name is a way of keeping you on track and reminding you of who you already are and who you are becoming. Dare to name that place where you, by God's grace, hope to be with God and all the saints and angels for eternity.

This week, spend time slowly and carefully considering the name of your spiritual home. One way to discover the name of your spiritual home this week is to reflect on four different things in your life: memories of thin spaces, memories of journeys, songs that have stirred your soul, and, finally, a word that has a sense of mystery.

Thin Spaces

The tagline for the church I serve is "a sacred space for your busy life." Our carpenter Gothic church, with its dim light, rosette window, dignified architecture, and warm wood, is a place that feels serene and holy. Whenever I am on the campus, I open the two sets of double doors so that people walking through the courtyard can look in the church and feel drawn in. One of my pleasures is to see people come into the church building and know that they are spending quiet time with God. Just as delightful is when, at drop-off or pick-up from the preschool on our campus, an exuberant child will drag their parents in for a few minutes of exploration in the wonderful space. I believe that when people of any age walk into the nave, they sense, at a level in their souls deeper than words, that this is a space where people have prayed for decades. People have cried and laughed, sat in deep silence, and sung to the rafters. The space is loved and worn-in, spiritually speaking. It is, in a small way, a thin space, an expression that describes when the boundary between heaven and earth feels thin.

What are the thin spaces in your life? The desk where I am writing these sentences is thin space for me. It is where I do my daily prayers, read the best spiritual writing I can find, and write most of my sermons. I can feel a difference between praying here at my desk at home versus a desk in a hotel when I am traveling or on vacation.

My friend Ru-Al is on Death Row. We write each other frequently and have occasional visits. One of the pillars of our friendship is our shared love of Christian spiritual practices. Like all the men of the Row, Ru-Al has a single cell. Twice a year, he takes his television and all of his books and art and puts them under his bed. Ordinarily, he loves going out onto the yard to shoot hoops, play dominoes, and hang out with his friends, but for a few weeks, he stays in his cell and keeps a monastic-like routine of prayer, fasting, and exercise. He always tells the guards ahead of time, so they won't be concerned that he's harming himself. In fact, it is just the opposite: he is strengthening his soul by deliberately converting his cell into a thin space. Furthermore, his behavior in prison has been clean enough that he could transfer from East Block, where the general population on the Row live, to North Seg, which houses the sixty-eight best-behaved men out of the 735 men at San Quentin. However, he chooses to stay in his current cell because, some years ago, the cell next to his was converted into an interfaith chapel where at least one group of men gathers to pray nearly every day. Knowing that he is next to a place of prayer feeds his soul and his sense of his own cell as a sacred space. He writes that he can "listen in on all the services. I must be the luckiest man on the Row then."[29]

A first step this week is to identify thin spaces in your life—the ones you currently enjoy and ones from the past. Remember the places in your life where you felt closest to God. Retreat centers, places of awesome natural beauty, and sublime sacred spaces are likely candidates. These places often hint at the glories of heaven and a peace and wholeness that passes all understanding. As you work toward naming your ultimate pilgrimage goal, spend some time remembering these spaces. I often think about three churches in the south of France called the Cistercian Sisters. Built in the twelfth century, they are simple, spare, elegant, and perfectly proportionate. Because of the simplicity of the spaces, I love to abide in them and imagine the generations of monks who prayed every day, seven times a day, in these spaces for centuries. If I spend enough time alone in the spaces, I can almost hear their voices. They are spaces where, in my imagination, I can hear the communion of saints in song.

I also go back in my imagination to two other retreat centers. In northeastern Massachusetts, Emery House is the retreat center of the Society of St. John the Evangelist, an Anglican monastic community of which I am a fellow. When I lived on the East Coast, I visited regularly. Today, I can easily call to mind an incredibly transformative experience when I stood at the end of a pier overlooking a pond. The nature I saw before me seemed to pulsate with divine life. Another special place for me is the Jesuit retreat center, where I took an eight-day Ignatian retreat just before I assumed the role of rector of St. Paul's. It was while I was thoughtfully pacing back and forth in a garden that I felt vividly and certainly that God would give me the authority I needed for God to do the work God wanted me to do at St. Paul's. Particularly in my early years as rector, as I encountered challenges and doubts, I often returned to that experience in the thin space of the Jesuit retreat center in Wernersville, Pennsylvania.

What have been the thin spaces that you have had the privilege of either visiting or living in for a season? Spend some time remembering. Your memories of those experiences give your mind rich food to chew on as you make your way to the name of your pilgrimage destination.

Journeys

Another set of memories to dwell on this week is to remember the times that you have been on your way from one place to another. The perfect expression of this is the spiritual pilgrimage like the one I made to Santiago de Campostela. On a pilgrimage, the entire point is to be someone who is on the way toward a spiritual home. There is no other work to be done but to slowly make our way toward home, preferably, although not exclusively, on our feet.

But we needn't have taken a spiritual pilgrimage to know what it is like to be in the in-between place of leaving a familiar setting to go to a new and unknown one. I've lived on the West Coast for more than twenty years but spent nearly all of my first thirty years on the East Coast, where I was born. In June of 1999, while my wife finished up her commitment as a therapist at a veterans' affairs hospital in Hartford, Connecticut, I got in a car by myself and drove across the country. Those five days of solo travel were an essential process of transition for me. At some level, I needed to see all the land that lay between the area I had always called home and this other place on this other ocean. I love to look at maps of the United States and to look out the window of airplanes as I cross our continent, but neither could be enough for me to capture the immensity of the shift I was going through as I relocated. I needed to register, hour by hour and close to the land, that this was all one country. The days of solo driving were what, in religious terms, is called "liminal time." For an adult preparing to be baptized at the Easter Vigil, Lent is often an intentionally liminal time with liturgical gestures that help the catechumen know that, while they aren't yet at the spiritual place they wish to be, they are on their way as a baptized Christian. Some churches will even give the catechumens some salt on their tongues right after the liturgy of the word and then dismiss them before the liturgy of the table, leaving them thirsty for more. Likewise, deliberate journeys of transition like my drive across the country, which, much to my surprise, I did mostly in silence, serve to whet the appetite for what lies ahead. I arrived in Los Angeles, ready to make a new home.

What have been the most meaningful journeys in your life? As you spend some time dwelling in your memories of those intentional transitions across landscapes, you begin to place in the center of your soul a pilgrim's heart.

Songs

Songs are among the most powerful expressions we have of naming a place where we yearn to go. Another way to nurture and attend to a pilgrim's heart is to remember the songs that make you long for a better place.

You might begin with hymns. Three hymns come to mind immediately for me. The first is often sung at funerals and offered me consolation at a worship service on the evening

---

of September 11, 2001. "O God, Our Help in Ages Past" is a gorgeous hymn. Its opening verse captures perfectly a life yearning for its pilgrim destination: "O God, our help in ages past, our hope for years to come, our shelter in the stormy blast, and our eternal home." In the music, the last phrase rises and then resolves perfectly on the final word, "home."

A second hymn that comes to mind begins, "Jerusalem, my happy home." This hymn is often sung at the time of communion, reminding us that the bread and wine we receive is a foretaste of the grand family meal of the heavenly banquet. This is one of the hymns I want at my funeral.

Finally, and most rousing of all, is Isaac Watts's great hymn, with its refrain: "We're marching to Zion, beautiful, beautiful Zion; we're marching upward to Zion, the beautiful city of God." As I've nurtured my own pilgrim's heart, this tune is the one that most often pops into my head in the course of an ordinary day, reminding me of who I am, and where, by God's grace, I want to be going.

We don't need to restrict our memories to hymns or other Christian tunes. The *a capella* group I sang with in college, the Society of Orpheus and Bacchus, has a stunning arrangement of the nineteenth-century American folk song, "Shenandoah." It begins with a solo voice singing, "O Shenandoah, I long to see you, away, you rolling river, O Shenandoah, I long to see you, away, I'm bound away, across the wide Missouri." The rest of the voices then gently come in and support the soloist with rich and gentle harmonies. At the end of the arrangement, the whole choir repeats "across the wide Missouri" in a passage that begins in unison and ends with a powerful and sumptuous chord sung in eight parts. The longing for Shenandoah concludes with a musical passage that expands the heart. I've never been to the Shenandoah of this song, but every time I sing or hear this song, my heart yearns to go there, like a pilgrim to his eternal home.[30]

What are your favorite hymns and songs that evoke a yearning for home, or a yearning for that better place? This week, make yourself a playlist, either in real life or just in your imagination, and use those tunes as a soundtrack not only as you name your spiritual home but also in the months ahead as you train the eyes of your spiritual heart to stay fixed on the consummation of your earthly pilgrimage.

Word

Finally, this week name your home. Settle on a name for the goal of your spiritual pilgrimage. Try to find a name that is, for you, the right blend of concrete and mystery. For example, a name that works well for me is "Zion." As I chew on that name in my mind, I find that it gives me all sorts of compelling flavors. To start, I think right away of the Isaac Watts hymn. This word appears often in scripture, giving me regular affirmation that Zion is a place where God is. Furthermore, the word Zion is often used interchangeably with the word Jerusalem as part of the Hebrew poetic style of repeating a word or thought in the next line. To pick one example among many, "Worship the LORD, O Jerusalem; praise your God, O Zion" (Psalm 147:13). The first and second halves of the verse mean the same thing but with words that have different connotations. I have been to Jerusalem, and while my associations with the name of the city are both earthly and heavenly, they are also of a noisy, crowded, stimulating, tense, and vibrant city that is in the state of Israel. Zion is the name of the mountain on which the city is built. My associations with that word are geographical and a little more abstract. I find it easier to keep the word Zion at a more exalted level and so use it as my name for my spiritual goal and my spiritual home.

Finally, when it comes to justice, my heart has always ached the most for justice and reconciliation between Blacks and Whites. I associate the name Zion with many predominantly Black churches I have seen and been in, and so I think of Zion as that place where the ultimate atonement of the American original sin of slavery, continued with Jim Crow and now mass incarceration, is finally atoned. Zion is my name for that home where the lie of race has no place.

Your word for home is likely to have multiple resonances that evoke the good things of God. The key is to find a word that gives a real, picturable goal and yet is not so restricted that it cannot connote multiple Christian images and desires. Some people have a single word they use their entire lives. Others are moved, for whatever reason, to make a change. The same may be true of your name for your spiritual home. Pick a word and stick with it for a long season of your life, allowing it to gain meaning and resonance slowly. And then, as is said in twelve-step programs, if the horse is dead, get off. Remember, we pray as we can—not as we cannot.

Finding and then abiding with a name for your ultimate spiritual home is one more sign that you are living with gladness and singleness of heart. A parishioner at a church where I used to serve once had the honor of being part of a small group of local business leaders who got to meet in person with the Rev. Billy Graham. At the end of their time together, Billy Graham said something to the effect of, "It's been an honor to spend time with you. I want you to know that I know where I am going to go after I die. If there is any doubt in your heart or mind, please don't leave this room until you have talked to me." I often wonder how I would have reacted had I been in that room. At the time I heard that story, my faith was still in its early stages. Would I have had the courage to stay and hopefully receive blessed assurance from Billy Graham? Now that my faith is stronger, I have followed Saint Augustine's lead who, though his faith was rock solid, knew that he did not and could not know his own ultimate fate. Augustine said that it is God who saves us, and we cannot save ourselves. Could even Billy Graham know his ultimate fate?

Yet surely the life of Billy Graham was filled with signposts that helped him know he was headed in the right direction. Along the Camino in northern Spain, faithful volunteers have painted an image of a yellow scallop shell, sometimes every few hundred yards if the way is tricky or confusing. If you spot a shell, you can be confident you are going in the right direction. The art of finding our own name for the spiritual home toward which we yearn is like a yellow scallop shell along the way. By grace, over time, as we continue steadily on the path toward our spiritual home, we might even be granted something like the fearless, generous, and loving faith of Billy Graham.

The good news is that you do not have to reinvent yourself or take on anything new to become a pilgrim. If you had been at that farmer's market outside Seattle, it is very likely that you too would have automatically tilted your face to the sun. It is how our bodies are built: we love the sun. Likewise, you too are a theotropic enigma, just like all PEOPLE, all the other faces on which you have gazed these last few weeks. You were made to tilt your whole life toward God and go toward being with God for eternity. You were made to be a pilgrim. With this final gentle practice, you give a name to the sun of your soul. We can imagine that what Jesus says to the paralytic in the Gospel of Mark, chapter 2, verse 11, he might now say to our pilgrim souls: "I say to you, stand up, take your mat, and go to your home."

THIS WEEK

Identify yourself as a pilgrim and give a name to your home, your ultimate destination.

SHIFT

Know in your heart, mind, and gut that you are headed toward your spiritual home.

REPETITION

At least once a day, name your home and consider how the gentle practices help you on your journey.

SABBATH PRAYER

O God, in your light we see light; help me reflect on the week that has passed, that I may remember in truth, and on the week to come, that I may be ready to do all such good works as thou hast prepared for me to walk in, in the name of Jesus, the light of the world. Amen.

Afterword

You are body and soul.

In this earthly life, we are always both body and soul. Where one ends and the other begins in us is a mystery. If you have ever been with someone at the moment that they died, you have had the experience of looking at the one you loved and knowing that the face is no longer that person. You could say something abstract like "vitality" has left that body, but from a Christian perspective, what has left the body is the soul. The soul, by grace, now abides with Jesus for eternity. Right now, as you read these words, you are both body and soul, and the one is not yet removed from the other. The gentle practices of this book are reliable and gentle ways to live as one whose body and soul are lovingly working in synch for your good and for the good of the world.

One way to more deeply connect the two is by identifying parts of our body as physical manifestations of the work of our soul. To do this requires imagination, but it can be a helpful tool in the pilgrim's way.

We begin this process as we began the book, with our feet.

For three weeks, without doubt or ambiguity, I was a pilgrim. Like many before me, I chose, with a friend, to walk the pilgrim way of the Via Francesca across northern Spain to Santiago de Campostela, the place where the church remembers that the Saint James the Apostle is buried. My friend and I met at an airport in New York, took a red-eye flight to Barcelona, and then a small plane to León, where, for the first and last time on the Camino, we stayed in a nice hotel. After a decent night of sleep, we got up early in the morning and made our way to the cathedral in León. In front of the church was a sign with a scallop shell, indicating that we had found the ancient Camino. Separately, we had been preparing for months for this moment. We had prayed, reflected, and talked. We had carefully collected and broken-in our equipment, and we had gradually built up the strength of our bodies. Now, at this moment, standing before this symbol of a shell, we were about to become pilgrims.

Our Camino boots were mostly ready for the journey. But, as I shared earlier in the book, my friend's boots were still too new. By the fourth day, his feet were covered in blisters, and he had to hobble along at half the pace for half the daily distance. By the sixth day, his feet toughened up, his boots were broken in, and we found the right mix of first aid.

Throughout the book, I encouraged you to consider twenty minutes of daily prayer and an hour each week of worship as the Camino boots of your soul. They support and sustain you on your spiritual journey. With these two practices well broken-in, you are prepared for new growth and spiritual maturity. Without prayer and worship, we stay hard of heart and unable to hear the still, small voice that is there, abiding in us.

This week, I invite you to place the prayer boot on one foot and the worship boot on the other. I am predominantly left-sided. I write and throw a ball with my left hand and kick a ball with my left foot. So, I put the inner work of prayer on my left foot, as that foot is the one that leads my body, and the daily practice of prayer is what leads the growth and strengthening of my soul. I am mostly, though, a balanced body. I swing a bat and play guitar like a right-handed person, and, the few times I've surfed or snowboarded, I've been "regular" and not "goofy-footed." My right foot is my foot of weekly worship. Amid the pandemic, it's the foot that aches most, as I can't share bread and wine with my Christian community. Once you've decided which foot wears which boot (prayer or worship), then I invite you to add the gentle practices to your body.

Strengthen Your Weak Knees

In the months leading up to that moment in front of the cathedral, I spent many hours walking. I began a habit of regular walking that has never left me. I knew, given the date and location of the start of our Camino, and the date and location of our return flight, that we would have to average about fifteen miles a day. In the months leading up to the Camino, my goal was to gradually become fit enough to tackle days like that with pleasure and confidence. It took a while, but I gradually built up my strength and endurance, at first finding five- and six-mile loops near my house and then ten- and twelve-mile hikes nearby. I could feel my body becoming fit and strong, the muscles on my legs taut, and a pleasant ache in my knees.

The book of Hebrews is written to encourage a Christian community whose enthusiasm is flagging. They are suffering the pushback and persecution of many of the early Christian communities, and the writer crafts a series of interconnected sermons to encourage them on their way. The book's climax is a vision of their destination. The writer piles on biblical names and descriptions of the goal of their earthly pilgrimage, including a mountain, a city, a feast, an assembly, and even Jesus himself (Hebrews 12:22-24). But to get to that great and mysterious place, a place ultimately beyond words, the pilgrim people require strong knees.

On our earthly pilgrimage, we strengthen our knees by inner work with scripture and outer work with a small group. Daily prayer for a Christian must include scripture. If you use Morning or Evening Prayer or pray the Daily Office from *The Book of Common Prayer*, you're already receiving your daily dose of scripture. Not only are you reading assigned passages from the lectionary, but also nearly every word and phrase of the entire *Book of Common Prayer* is derived from the Bible. For those who pray extemporaneously, be sure to supplement the silence with at least the Lord's Prayer, a psalm, and a brief passage of scripture. Scripture is the living word, and we must come to its words often so that we can draw on its strength. The knee of our soul needs the power of scripture to move us forward on the way.

We often do best when we are part of a band of pilgrims. There may be some seasons of our lives when we are called to be alone for a time, but they are the exception, not the rule. A small group lends us the support and wisdom of others who are on the way. We learn and are inspired by the struggles and successes of others. If scripture strengthens our knee on the side of our body of the inner journey, a small band of fellow pilgrims strengthens the knee of our soul on the side of our body dedicated to the outer journey. With prayer, worship, scripture, and our small group, the legs of our soul are strong, steady, and ready to carry us onward.

Bear One Another's Burdens

One of the most crucial ways to prepare for pilgrimage is to carefully prepare your backpack. The largest and heaviest item is likely to be a sleeping bag, and the trick is to find one that's heavy enough to keep you warm on the coolest nights without being so heavy that it adds needless weight. When it comes to the other essential items, some pilgrims go so far as to break the handle off of the toothbrush to save a little bit of weight. I wasn't nearly that obsessive and was able to create a fully stocked pack that weighed under fifteen pounds. In the last stage of my preparation for the Camino, I filled my new backpack with fifteen pounds of random stuff and took to the longest trails near my home so I could practice with the extra weight.

On the Camino, everything my shoulders carried helped me thrive on the journey. By contrast, the shoulders of our soul are there to bear the burdens of others. Paul admonishes in his letter to the Galatians to "bear one another's burdens, and in this way (we) fulfill the law of Christ" (Galatians 6:2). In the gentle practice of using our wound, I encourage care and intentionality in the amount and type of suffering we choose to take on, both of ourselves and on behalf of others.

On one shoulder of bearing one another's burdens is financial generosity, supporting my church and other organizations with the gifts I have been given. On the other shoulder is service. This shoulder reminds me to carve out an hour a week to be with my neighbors who are the least, on the margins or poor. With one shoulder we give away money, with the other shoulder we give away time.

Place the Gentle Practices in Your Side and Head

The gentle practice of use your wound has already been placed in our side and heart. We are to leave the wound open and, at the same time, be careful and attentive, ensuring that the loving wound does not become infected with bitterness or resentment. The wound is a gentle reminder that true love hurts. If the wound in the side is upheld by strong pilgrim legs and is in coordination with strong pilgrim shoulders that bear the burdens of others, it is more likely to stay healthy and loving.

The other gentle practices are placed in our head. The gentle practice of looking at each face is a practice of stewardship of the eyes. We look with a deeper appreciation at the PERSON in front of us, remembering that they are made in the image and likeness of God. Other practices occur between our ears—and with our mouths. Saying and remembering that the work is very near us and the practice of naming each work calls upon the human power, first given to Adam, to name. By using the power of words, we slow down and attend to what we are doing. As we become adept at these practices, we can become poets of our daily life. The weekly time of praying and reflecting on the sabbath invites us to think in the light of Christ and so remember and plan with graceful freedom.

Finally, smiling our secret smile uses the muscle memory around our mouths to remind us of the gift of Beauty and to dwell in gratitude. In this last stage of integration, we can both remember the name of our pilgrimage destination—heaven, Zion, Jerusalem, whatever it may be—and smile our secret smile. We trust that the joys that await us are far beyond anything we can ask or imagine. Our pilgrim goal is the very best reason to smile.

We can now imagine our bodies and souls are on their pilgrim way, every day, making their way toward our spiritual home with Jesus. My prayer is that each of us will know that God sends us out into the world every day to continue and deepen God's work of atonement. I pray that when Jesus says in the Gospel of John, "Very truly, I tell you, the one who believes in me will also do the works that I do and, in fact, will do greater works than these" (John 14:12), we not only know what he means, but also we can confidently point to actions in our lives that are works not just of this world but of the world to come. The goal is that we move through our ordinary days with gladness and singleness of heart and act in ways that partake of the glory of our eternal home.

Guide to the Weekly Practices

Week 1

The Work Is Very Near You

Pray: O God, send me this day to do the work you have given me to do, to love and serve you with gladness and singleness of heart. *Amen.*

Gentle Practice: In times of transition, think to yourself: "The work is very near you."

Words: Work, Send, Gentle

Shift: Identify as your call whatever work God would have you do next.

Repetition: Choose three daily times of transition in your ordinary day and, this week, say to yourself, "The work is very near you," each time you are in that place and time of transition.

Camino Boots: Commit to weekly worship and twenty minutes of prayer.

Week 2

Look at Each Face

Gentle Practice: Look at each face and remember that they are a PERSON.

Words: Gladness, PERSON, Theotropic, Enigma

Shift: Practice stewardship of your eyes, particularly around people.

Repetition: Each day, attend to the faces you see regularly such as family, friends, and co-workers, and remember that each one is a PERSON.

Camino Boots: Commit to weekly worship and twenty minutes of prayer.

Pray Each Day: O God, send me this day to do the work you have given me to do, to love and serve you with gladness and singleness of heart. *Amen.*

Week 3

Name Each Work

Gentle Practice: Name each work and so learn to mindfully do one thing at a time.

Words: Singleness, Repetition, Conviction

Shift: Release the temptation to multitask.

Repetition: Choose an activity you do every day, like making breakfast, and name each distinct action.

Camino Boots: Commit to weekly worship and twenty minutes of prayer.

Pray Each Day: O God, send me this day to do the work you have given me to do, to love and serve you with gladness and singleness of heart. *Amen.*

Week 4

Pray and Reflect on the Sabbath

Pray on the Sabbath: O God, in your light we see light; help me reflect on the week that has passed, that I may remember in truth, and on the week to come, that I may be ready to do all such good works as thou hast prepared for me to walk in, in the name of Jesus, the light of the world. *Amen.*

Gentle Practice: On Sunday, before worship, say the above prayer and then reflect on the last week and the week to come.

Words: Reflection, Source, Light, House, Mirror, Vineyard, Sabbath

Shift: Reclaim the biblical teaching of the sabbath and use it to integrate the gentle practices into your life.

Repetition: Once a week, at the same time and in the same place, take ten minutes to reflect.

Camino Boots: Commit to weekly worship and twenty minutes of prayer.

Pray Each Day: O God, send me this day to do the work you have given me to do, to love and serve you with gladness and singleness of heart. *Amen.*

Week 5

Smile Your Secret Smile

Gentle Practice: Find your unique angelic smile and, when no one is looking, smile your secret smile, remembering that life is beautiful.

Words: Heart, Smile, Beauty, Gratitude, Acedia

Shift: Have faith that Beauty, Truth, and Goodness are real—and that our world participates in all three.

Repetition: Regularly, throughout each day, notice Beauty and always give thanks to God.

Camino Boots: Commit to weekly worship and twenty minutes of prayer.

Pray Each Day: O God, send me this day to do the work you have given me to do, to love and serve you with gladness and singleness of heart. *Amen.*

Pray on the Sabbath: O God, in your light we see light; help me reflect on the week that has passed, that I may remember in truth, and on the week to come, that I may be ready to do all such good works as thou hast prepared for me to walk in, in the name of Jesus, the light of the world. *Amen.*

Week 6

Use Your Wound

Gentle Practice: Imagine that you have an open wound in your side, like the resurrected Jesus, and that, just as God sent Jesus wounded, we are sent wounded. We are to use our wounds.

Words: Send Me, Open Wound, Sorrow

Shift: Do not be afraid to feel pain and sorrow, trusting that God will use your wounded heart to bring healing and love.

Repetition: Find times of quiet to identify the ache in your heart and feel, without words or judgment, the simple feeling of sorrow.

Camino Boots: Commit to weekly worship and twenty minutes of prayer.

Pray Each Day: O God, send me this day to do the work you have given me to do, to love and serve you with gladness and singleness of heart. *Amen*.

Pray on the Sabbath: O God, in your light we see light; help me reflect on the week that has passed, that I may remember in truth, and on the week to come, that I may be ready to do all such good works as thou hast prepared for me to walk in, in the name of Jesus, the light of the world. *Amen*.

Week 7

Name Your Home

Gentle Practice: Identify yourself as a pilgrim and give a name to your home, your ultimate destination.

Words: Pilgrim, Home, Thin Place, Journey, Songs, Word

Shift: Know in your heart, mind and gut that you are headed toward your spiritual home.

Repetition: At least once a day, do a mental check of your body, from feet to head, placing the practices in the appropriate places.

Camino Boots: Commit to weekly worship and twenty minutes of prayer.

Pray Each Day: O God, send me this day to do the work you have given me to do, to love and serve you with gladness and singleness of heart. *Amen.*

Pray on the Sabbath: O God, in your light we see light; help me reflect on the week that has passed, that I may remember in truth, and on the week to come, that I may be ready to do all such good works as thou hast prepared for me to walk in, in the name of Jesus, the light of the world. *Amen.*

Notes

1   Samuel Taylor Coleridge, *The Major Works including Biographia Literaria* (New York: Oxford University Press, 1985), 666.

2   Catherine Pickstock, *Repetition and Identity* (Oxford: Oxford University Press, 2013), 97.

3   John Chapman, *Spiritual Letters* (New York: Burns & Oates, 2003), 25.

4   *The Book of Common Prayer*, 1979, 339.

5   Cited in Martin Laird, *Into the Silent Land* (New York: Oxford University Press, 2006), 37-38.

6   W. H. Auden, *Collected Poems* (New York: Vintage Books, 1991), 692.

7   Coleridge, 666.

8   Admiral William H. McRaven, *Make Your Bed: Little Things that Can Change Your Life...And Maybe the World* (New York: Hachette Book Group, 2017), 6.

9   *The Rule of St. Benedict in English* (Collegeville: The Liturgical Press, 1982), 55.

10 Søren Kierkegaard, *Upbuilding Discourses in Various Spirits* (Princeton: Princeton University Press, 1993), 70.

11 Ibid., 70.

12 Ibid., 121.

13 Malcolm Guite, *Mariner: A Voyage with Samuel Taylor Coleridge* (London: Hodder & Stoughton, 2017), 260.

14 Coleridge, 93.

15   Samuel Taylor Coleridge, *The Collected Works of Samuel Taylor Coleridge: Aids to Reflection, Volume Nine,* (Princeton: Princeton University Press, 1993) xcv.

16   Ibid., 22.

17   Ibid., xciv.

18   Ibid., 15-16.

19   Ibid., xcii.

20   Quoted in Robert Calasso *The Celestial Hunter* (New York: Farrar, Straus, & Giroux, 2020), 396.

21   Coleridge, *Aids to Reflection*, 202.

22   George Herbert, *The Country Parson, The Temple* (New Jersey: Paulist Press, 1981), 120.

23   Evagrius Ponticus, *The Praktikos & Chapters On Prayer* (Collegeville: Liturgical Press, 1972), 18-19.

24   Ibid., 19.

25   Søren Kierkegaard, *Papers and Journals: A Selection* (London: Penguin Books, 1996), 188.

26   *The Book of Common Prayer*, 134. You can hear a later recording of the All Saints' Beverly Hills Choir singing the anthem at https://www.youtube.com/watch?v=L1n0RZ8WmQQ

27   Pickstock, 147.

28   *The Philokalia: The Complete Text, Volume One* (London: Faber and Faber, 1979), 252.

29   Albert "Ru-Al" Jones, *Put on the Shelf to Die*, unpublished and forthcoming.

30   The arrangement of "Shenandoah" can be heard at https://www.youtube.com/watch?v=AZ4UtUezn7s

About the Author

Christopher H. Martin is the rector of St. Paul's, San Rafael, a parish in the Diocese of California where he has served since 2004. He previously served parishes in Los Angeles and Hartford, Connecticut. He is the founder of The Restoration Project, a national movement of churches devoted to spiritual maturity through seven core Christian practices. He is the author of the book, *The Restoration Project*, also published by Forward Movement, as well as a variety of articles and reviews. He received both his bachelor of arts and master of divinity degrees from Yale. He married his college sweetheart, and they have two sons.

About Forward Movement

Forward Movement is committed to inspiring disciples and empowering evangelists. Our ministry is lived out by creating resources such as books, small-group studies, apps, and conferences.

Our daily devotional, *Forward Day by Day*, is also available in Spanish (Adelante *Día a Día*) and Braille, online, as a podcast, and as an app for smartphones or tablets. It is mailed to more than fifty countries, and we donate nearly tens of thousands of copies each quarter to prisons, hospitals, and nursing homes.

We actively seek partners across the church and look for ways to provide resources that inspire and challenge. A ministry of the Episcopal Church for more than eighty years, Forward Movement is a nonprofit organization funded by sales of resources and by gifts from generous donors.

To learn more about Forward Movement and our resources, visit ForwardMovement.org. We are delighted to be doing this work and invite your prayers and support.